going somewhere out of town/province /country we check out the Derby scene and are invited with open arms.

I've been bullied,tossed around, ridiculed and put down REPEATEDLY. I was kinda gunshy at first. I'm So happy to make so many brothers and sisters from so many places."

Zapped Wylde

"This is derby."

"Derby Adds Quality to Life."

"It had a strong enough impact i started my own league."

"I'm more social and have met some really lovely women. I love roller derby derby because whenever I put skates on I laugh and smile."

"Derby has changed ever aspect of my life...for the better!!! Socially, emotionally, physically and...well maybe not financially LOL. I have met new people and became great friends. My job (social worker) is an emotional roller coaster. Derby is a great outlet for the anxiety and frustration. Derby IS my midlife crisis :)"

"It has helped me resist 'giving in' to a sense of a weakening body. I was growing chronically tired...so that I could keep up with my garden or other things that were important to me. Derby has given me an outlet to feel strong again."

"I am fitter, thinner, and have a better social life than ever before, and I am about to turn 46!"

"A number of things changed at about the same time as I started Derby - I had a Gastric Sleeve surgery which meant I dropped about

20kg (45 pounds) over a 3 month period - I tell every body that asks that the weight loss is due to Derby :-)"

"I am a stay at home Mom with two boys, the youngest one is Autistic. I was becoming depressed with my 'normal' life, and didn't have many female friends. I went to one Derby bout with my hubby, and fell in love. I started as Fresh Meat and just took my Level 1 assessments. I am a much happier person now, and I am enjoying all my new family."

"Not yet but it is changing (sorry i am frensh)."

"It has helped me build confidence to stand up for myself not be pushed over, which has been a difficulty. I don't apologize as much any more :)"

"I started at 47 hoping the exercise would help with my hot flashes. I had a stroke three months later that took most of my eye sight. Through it all the women have always been there. I'm much older than they are and some times that can be awkward, but when the shit hits the fan we're there for each other. We're family. That's beautiful."

"I'm feeling better, both physically and mentally, than before I started skating (at 38) thanks to roller derby."

"I started derby at 45 and fell in love with the sport. It is the only exercise I have been able to stay committed to and I rarely miss a practice. I feel strong, fit, and empowered and try to pass the sport onto others."

"Derby has changed my life in so many positive ways. Keeps me very fit, challenged mentally, physically and socially. It makes me step

"I'm 49 years old and during the day i have a high powered job with lots of stress.

I love roller derby because it takes me away from my job, and gives me an outlet. (this is the only outlet that I have found that totally absorbs me.)

I am one of the weaker players because of my age and i have physical restraints of age and fitness. However derby has rewound my life by 20 years. I have suffered with back pain and disc problems for my whole life-(since age 18). Since derby i have no issues. (3 yrs ago I was on walking sticks for 4 months!).

Derby really hasn't saved my life – it's given me one!!"

"So...I just turned 46.

I used to skate all the time when I was a kid but stopped when I moved away from home back in 1988. Back in March 2014 a much younger friend of mine told me that she had checked out a roller derby team here where I live. Not knowing what the history was of the sport in my town I assumed it was at the roller rink 1.5 blocks from my house.

So after not having donned skates for some 25ish years, I decided to take my teenage son and go check out the rink during an open session. Within the first 30 minutes I had realized how much I missed the feeling and freedom that being on skates gave me when I was younger. So off to talk to the owner of the rink to see about getting a pair of my own skates (just to have them for leisure skating at open sessions).

I ordered my skates and agreed to come to my first derby practice...little did I know that this was not the same team my friend had been talking about. This was a new team just starting out and just building their team from scratch and definitely the right team for me.

Now I have been skating with our team for some 9 months and love it. I am riddled with health troubles, diabetes related issues and strength issues from complications of the disease and a couple minor injuries, and had never imagined being this active again.

I may never be strong enough again to skate in my first official bout and I may never be able to get strong enough to pass my minimum skills test but the sense of family and community that I have found has made me want to try to get better every day...even knowing that my future in derby may only be as Ref or NSO I am totally ok with it...I love my derby family and the sense of belonging and empowerment it has given me to be stronger and better every day."

Granny Smith, #29 - Poison Apples Roller Derby

"My Girlfriend wanted to start a Derby league, here in Cochrane Ontario Canada. She spoke to a ladie from Sault Saint Marie (Laura DevilsOwn Houle). She told my GF that there was another woman trying to start a league in our little town.

My GF get on the phone with her and it was someone she worked with for years!!!

Brainstorming leads to the first team meeting, almost 20 people showed up.

I've never done too much in sports,but I knew I'd really love this sport, Then I was nominated Assistant Coach. I Loved it! I couldn't believe what was happening.

The head coach and I spoke, the girls listened, the team grew so fast...safety / commitment / determination. I needed MORE. I Hopped into REFFING.

I was never too good at reading books, but this was very different. With every page turned, knowledge was built and was helping me as a coach as well.... But,I wanted MORE!!! Just this year, Timmins Ontario hosted the very first CO-ED Scrimmage in northern Ontario. I could not believe my eyes. "Are you kiddin' me??? Let me in!!!" I Played in the CoEd scrimmage and reffed the following game.

I simply don't know how to explain how Roller Derby has changed my life. I've been 100% invited to/from every team around. If we're outside of my comfort zone. I have become a much more confident person. I feel strong. I have lots of new friends. I am very happy!"

"I never played a sport before. I never experienced team bonding before derby. I have been a derby fan since 1968 and always fantasized about being a skater so ten years ago when Pioneer Valley Roller Derby started the first men's team, it was like a lifelong dream come true. It happened at a particularly low point in my life and really saved me from a depressive state."

"It hasn't changed my life but has certainly enriched it! I've meant some wonderful people over the years. Also since being part of a league is about running a nonprofit organization; the roles I have served has helped equip me for the responsibilities I have as a new business owner."

"Never been stronger, Valley, or more confident since derby."

"It reminded me of the athlete that I used to be, and now am again!"

"For years I wanted to try out Derby. I always love to skate, but I didn't know if I had what it would take to actually be able to skate Derby style. At 46 I decided to go ahead and go to my first practice. I was really nervous, I realized I didn't know how to skate anymore, since last time I was on skates was 30 years ago. but the love, camaraderie, friendly atmosphere and like minded people made it a great experience. Though I have never had that passion to be a truly competitive skater, or to live and breathe Derby, like some, I feel that I have found the most wonderful sport, and the most genuine people I've ever known in my life. I have made true friends, with a common interest, even though our lives might be totally different, and our other life interests might be totally different, we all come together for one reason, and that's to skate. I am more confident, outgoing,

and have a higher desire to just live life to thenfullest, because I know when everything is going crappy, I could just strap on my skates, call up a bunch of my derby friends, and go have a good time, laugh and love."

"Helped me leave a bad relationship."

"Derby is the best therapy ever! It keeps me in shape, makes me continue to challenge myself and constantly push my limitations. It requires teamwork. The best skater in the world can't win alone; you don't necessarily have to like or get along with every skater on your team outside of derby; but once you are on the track, you have to have each other's backs, and operate as a team in order to be effective. Also, I did get lucky and met my Derby Love (she was the coach of one of the teams I played against... now she is my team mate). . . And much much more which doesn't really have words... it is an overwhelming mixture of physical and mental and emotional and chemical and.... which floods every cell during and after derby... only one way to experience it...."

"Before derby I had not lasted a season in any organised sport for over 20 years. My confidence and health have improved thanks to the regular exercise. I have recently completed a coaching accreditation course. I can see my association with derby continuing long after my competitive skating days are over, I plan to work towards becoming an official."

"Community. Confidence. Fitness."

"Met great new friends."

"Made me a stronger woman; mental as well as physically."

"Derby bright a new light to my life. As a mom of three kids was beginning to feel as if I needed something for just me. Derby has given me that. I love skating. I love getting stronger and better. I love that I'm 45 and I have a lot of energy and in it slowing down any time soon."

"It gave me the physical and mental outlet I needed. It has had many ups and downs but more ups to keep me from walking away or retirement. I want to help grow the sport."

"Best thing I ever did."

"I am more outgoing, and in better shape. Participating in roller derby has made me realize I am able to do things I am afraid of or challenged by."

"Derby has allowed me to see other cities in both the US and abroad."

"I have accomplished things I've ne thought I was physically capable of!"

Starting and Coaching a Roller Derby League

Donna Kay

Starting and Coaching a Roller Derby League

Copyright © 2024 by Donna Kay

All Rights Reserved

No part of this book may be reproduced or transmitted in any form or by any means, electronic or mechanical, including photocopying, recording, or by any information storage and retrieval system without the written permission of the author, except where permitted by law.

Cover photo: Eric Lyons Photography, University Place, WA

Dedicated to my good friend and one & only 'derby wife' Jerry Seltzer (June 3, 1932 - July 1, 2019).

Acknowledgments

I'd like to acknowledge all of the amazing people who have paid it forward throughout the years. I've been lucky to have encountered more than my share of derby love from skaters across the USA. Here's to the true athletes and people who are kind.

www.derbyover40.com.

Introduction

During a rough patch in my life, I realized that Roller Derby was my vehicle to find an identity at a time when I most needed it. It ultimately became much more than that.

After a lifetime of feeling objectified (including self-objectification), derby became a way to let me experience my power. I entered into it with a lot of insecurity, as many skaters do, but wound up feeling proud that I could get stronger and faster as an older person.

I had pretty much been resigned to the fact that, as an older skater, I would never have the endurance I might have had 20 or 30 years ago. I accepted that I would have limitations. I made the decision to learn to maneuver better and smarter and work on having my head in the game. This approach made sense to me because I could be an asset to the stronger players by increasing my confidence. My goal was to help empower my teammates rather than compare myself to them. Before I knew it, I was skating faster, getting lower, and learning to play derby.

I was obsessed with derby but realized I was much more interested in building strength and fascinated by skater behavior, specifically women. Derby is only one of many venues for women to find power, but I'm pretty sure it's the only sport that is most often used to create an entire identity through participation. I don't think it is a coincidence that it is mostly women skaters out there.

For me, derby has been a quest to find ways to share empowerment with a focus on self-esteem and a vehicle to overcome life's challenges. My interest in derby as a community sport has been because of this piece, the psychological aspect, and the profound impact it IS (not appears to be) making on the participants.

In my observation, a lot of people in competition view the success of their peers as a threat. Imagine if we could change that for a few people; imagine the real power that could come of that. As a whole, we could be unstoppable and create teams that would be completely awe-inspiring across the board.

Roller Derby is extraordinary, especially so for the people who are part of it. The empowerment it brings to participants is no secret, which sets this sport apart from all others. It is a fitness outlet, a social outlet, an identity, a community, and, for an unknown percentage, a culture. For the competitive athlete, it is a dream come true or could be a dream come true. The same goes for people looking for community, having a social life, or a fitness outlet. For many skaters, it is the first chance to participate in a sport or have any sort of mind-body experience. Above all, it is an opportunity for self-growth and confidence.

It is unlikely that there exists any other sport with as diverse a population as Roller Derby. Participants range from students, doctors, men, women, young, old, sports enthusiasts, misfits, cheerleaders, superstars, bullies, and leaders. It is both defensive and offensive at the same time and requires a strong commitment to gain the skills needed to become an advanced skater.

The diversity brings what is known as derby drama[1]. It also brings group efficacy and a derby "high" that is hard to find outside of being a professional athlete.

---

[1] Derby Drama is a common phrase in the derby community, that is gossip resulting from people who have (most likely) never played sports in their lives, and don't understand that starting lineups are typically made up of more advanced skaters, among other things. Roller Derby is like a magnet for bullies. So....

A tricky aspect is dealing with how to give everyone enough skating time to earn a place on the roster. One approach is to treat this sport as a mainstream venue that allows people to learn to skate and gain skills while allowing athletes to work together in groups of similar skills. The anxiety that goes along with Roller Derby is preventable and exactly the opposite of what this sport can and should bring to people everywhere. Good places to introduce Roller Derby as a sport if there are no skating rinks available are schools, city park departments, or community centers.

When I started skating, I watched what was happening and became fascinated at how Roller Derby impacts lives. I credit derby for literally saving me more than once, and I've heard this story many times over. I've seen skaters leave in tears (myself included) for not being invited onto a team or league for vague reasons. Even when my skills grew and I was on a committee to evaluate new skaters, I couldn't identify what the criteria were for telling someone they could not be a Roller Derby skater.

I began teaching derby in Seattle parks and at a local community college. My objective was to:

1). Mainstream the sport and make it accessible for

anyone to learn.

2). Help people have the opportunity to learn.

3). Create a job for myself to be able to do something that makes a difference.

4). Create opportunities for others.

Pay it forward and share the freaking love, ok? And if that isn't possible, just shut up and skate. It is important to look carefully at our own agenda about why we are involved and share the belief that there is a place for anyone and everyone. If you are offended, please read my guide for starting and coaching a derby league with a strong emphasis on the mental game.

Entity Choices

(Not applicable for someone not in the US). If you are on a shoestring budget or don't have funds to hire someone to expertly and legally set up your league, it is possible to do the filing on your own to get started. BUT...setting up a company and the entity you choose is a big decision that will have long-term implications, so research this on your own before you do anything. After you decide the route you'd like to take, talk it over with an attorney or CPA. Do your research, but legwork before your first meeting with someone will save you a lot of money.

My adult leagues were for profit, and originally, I had them structured as a C-corporation. Eventually, the State of Washington allowed for a new entity structure called an SPC (Social Purpose Corporation). An SPC allows a for-profit corporation the latitude to have a greater mission than profit. It must either be about environmental sustainability or benefit the community. Often, it goes hand in hand with a non-profit, which we formed as a subsidiary corporation. This 501C3 has the mission of mainstreaming Roller Derby, funding a facility for our league, community outreach, and organizing events.

Again, I emphasize that I'm not an attorney and wouldn't recommend making a decision without your own research and gaining awareness of the pros and cons of your situation, but here is the overview in a nutshell. Also, know where you live will factor into the following entity choices with variances from state to state.

Essentially, the entity you choose will determine the tax returns you need to file. Of course, it will also play a part in how protected you are from personal liability, how you raise funds, and how you ultimately present your league to your community.

Check the state you live in; there are always helpful websites and links that can walk you through filing and necessary requirements and other resources. Check the resource section of this book for a list of numbers and websites for your state.

Sole Proprietorship

A sole proprietorship is a business that is owned by one person. The income and expenses (usually a schedule C) are reported on a personal income tax return with a personal social security number for tax reporting. Forming a sole proprietorship is a simple way to own a business, but the risk is high. The owner's personal assets are at risk and the liability for an individual is high. Even though I'm not an attorney and can't give legal advice, this one is somewhat of a no-brainer. I'm going to go out on a limb and be bold enough to tell you not to choose a sole proprietorship for your Roller Derby league. This entity is NOT a good idea for a Roller Derby league.

Corporations

A corporation is owned by shareholders (usually active in management), but it CAN be owned by a single individual who can serve as the director and as the required officer, too. Without an admin team to help you, there are a lot of pieces here to tend to. Strive to create a team/board and be aware that they might not be knocking your door down to help you.

Typically, there is a board of directors elected by the shareholders. All of the day-to-day tasks are performed by the officers appointed by the board. If one of the shareholders should die, their shares are transferred to their heirs, but it doesn't mean the corporation would "die."

A C-corporation is taxed as a separate legal entity with the profits taxed when they are earned AND any dividends paid to shareholders will have their distributions taxed too, so as you can see, this is being taxed twice.

If you are a corporation and opt (this is an extra task that needs to be initiated by someone; it doesn't happen all by itself) to be taxed as an S corporation, that means you can function as a corporation but can be taxed as individuals.

Ok, this is important. S-corporation's losses flow

through to the shareholders and can be deducted on their personal taxes, BUT profits earned by the company will be reported on the individual's income regardless of any cash amounts distributed TO them. These profits and losses are allocated based on share ownership for tax purposes, so think about how many shares to authorize when you get set up and who will get them. ISSUING the shares is another step down the line. Just because they are authorized doesn't mean they've been issued. Usually, S-corporations don't pay income taxes and the liability for the profits is passed on to the shareholders on their individual returns (with limitations).

Keeping it simple. You probably don't want to authorize a zillion shares. I kept mine at 1,000 with the intention of giving some away, retaining some to sell in the future, and reserving some for future employee stock options. Even though my league was "by the skater for the skater," I wanted to make a profit and pay people who worked in and for my company. I believed I could have "volunteer" volunteers and not have committee work be mandatory. Eventually, I hoped to weed out volunteers entirely (for the adult leagues, not the non-profit) and pay everyone who worked for the company.

I intended to reinvest a good percentage of my profits into the company to expand the IT/website and reserve a percentage for the scholarship fund that initially compelled me to earn money from the sport's growth. The fund was earmarked to help all skaters (not just my leagues) with league dues, gear, funds for insurance, etc. We provided gear and travel expenses for our travel team and paid the refs and NSOs.

A Roller Derby league fits the IRS description of a social club, but the requirements for filing differ from state to state. You can find the filing forms online; a list is included in this book that can help you find the website and information for your state.

IN BRIEF, here are the requirements:

The club must be organized for exempt purposes, i.e., organized for pleasure, recreation, and other similar purposes. You must have bylaws or a written policy about non-discrimination. The club can't exceed the safe harbor guidelines, meaning that 35% of GROSS receipts can be from non-member sources, including individual investment income. No more than 15% can come from non-member use of club facilities and services. If you exceed the guidelines, they will evaluate whether you can remain a non-profit, so 15% - 35% is known as safe harbors.

You need to keep good records and hang onto them for three years. Stay within the limits of non-member income. Even though a league has tax-exempt status, it may still need to file taxes on income received outside of its members. If you have more than $1,000 from an unrelated business, you'll need to file a TRS form 990-T and an annual exempt organization form. The club needs to provide an opportunity for "personal contact," and no, we're not talking about hitting. This is handled by having practices and meetings. You need to have members and charge membership fees. If your league is open to the public and even non-members can come in, this could be problematic. If you hold fundraisers that are open to the public, do your research first. Other than reasonable salaries paid for administration, the overall club can't be for the gain of one person. If your club provides ongoing services to the general public for money, it is not non-profit.

Use caution and due diligence when holding fund-raising activities, and ensure you have someone who can handle the legal and tax filing for your league.

My vision fell apart after a year-long battle with breast cancer when I had to be out for six weeks on four different occasions during the year. My guest coaches often poached my skaters and then the derby drama began with (untrue) rumors of my not paying facilities and other nebulous gripes. What they didn't know was that I invested $30,000 of my own money to get the league started, including paying facility rentals out of my own pocket before the income was enough to cover it. My efforts to be able to reclaim some of the startup funds were misinterpreted. I am telling you this because you need to be careful. Despite having the vision to make the world a better place, rumors can wipe you out. Jeesh!

Before breast cancer - falling down, after breast cancer - getting up.

Links for Secretaries of State

ALABAMA 334-242-7200

http://www.sos.state.al.us/

ALASKA 907-465-2530

http://www.commerce.state.ak.us/occ

ARIZONA 602-542-3230

http://www.azsos.gov/

ARKANSAS 01-682-101

http://www.sosweb.state.ar.us/

California 916-653-3795

http://www.sos.ca.gov

COLORADO 303-894-2251

http:/www.sos.state.co.us/

CONNECTICUT 203-566-3216

http://www.sots.state.ct.us/

DELAWARE 302-739-4111

http://www.state.de.us/sos

DC 202-727-7278

https://os.dc.gov/

FLORIDA 904-488-9000

http://www.dos.state.fl.us/

GEORGIA 04-656-2817

http://www.sos.state.ga.us/

GUAM GOVT N/A

http://ns.gov.gu/

HAWAII 808-586-2727

http://www.hawaii.gov/ltgov/

ILLLINOIS 217-782-7880

http://www.sos.state.il.us/

INDIANA 317-232-6576

https://www.in.gov/sos/

IOWA 515-281-5204

http://www.sos.state.ia.us/

KANSAS 913-293-2236

http://www.kssos.org/

KENTUCKY 502-564-2848

http://www.sos.ky.gov/

LOUISIANA 504-925-4704

http://www.sec.state.la.us/

MAINE 207-287-3676

http://www.state.me.us/sos/

MARYLAND 410-225-1330

http://www.sos.state.md.us/

MASSACHUSETTS 617-727-9640

http://www.state.ma.us/sec/

MICHIGAN 517-334-6206

http://www.michigan.gov/sos

MINNESOTA 612-296-2803

http://www.state.mn.us/ebranch/sos/

MISSISSIPPI 601-359-1333

http://www.sos.state.ms.us/

MISSOURI 314-751-1310

http://www.sos.mo.gov/

MONTANA 406-444-3665

http://sos.mt.gov/

NEBRASKA 402-471-4079

http://www.nol.org/home/SOS/

NEVADA 7 02-687-5203

http://sos.state.nv.us/

NEW HAMPSHIRE 6 03-271-3242

http://www.sos.nh.gov/

NEW JERSEY 609-530-6400

http://www.state.nj.us/state/

NEW MEXICO 505-827-4508

http://www.sos.state.nm.us/

NEW YORK 518-474-4752

http://www.dos.state.ny.us/

NORTH CAROLINA 919-733-4201

http://www.secstate.state.nc.us/

NORTH DAKOTA 701-328-4282

http://www.state.nd.us/sec/

OHIO 14-466-3910

http://www.state.oh.us/sos/

OKLAHOMA 05-521-3911

http://www.sos.state.ok.us/

OREGON 503-986-2200

http://www.sos.state.or.us/

PENNSYLVANIA 717-787-1057

http://www.dos.state.pa.us/

PUERTO RICO 787-722-2121

http://www.estado.gobierno.pr/

RHODE ISLAND 401-277-2357

http://www.state.ri.us/

SOUTH CAROLINA 803-734-2158

http://www.scsos.com/

SOUTH DAKOTA 605-773-4845

http://www.state.sd.us/sos/sos.htm

TENNESSEE 615-741-2286

http://www.state.tn.us/sos/

TEXAS 512-463-5555

http://www.sos.state.tx.us/

UTAH 801-530-4849

http://www.utah.gov/ltgovernor/

VERMONT 802-828-2386

http://www.sec.state.vt.us/

VIRGIN ISLANDS 340-776-8515

http://www.ltg.gov.vi/

VIRGINIA 804-371-9141

http://www.commonwealth.virginia.gov

WASHINGTON 360-725-0377

http://www.secstate.wa.gov/

WEST VIRGINIA 304-558-8000

http://www.wvsos.com/

WISCONSIN 608-266-3590

http://www.sos.state.wi.us/

WYOMING 307-777-7311 http://soswy.state.wy.us/

Note: All drills in the warm-ups and throughout the book can be modified to accommodate beginners and advanced skaters alike.

Roller Derby Coaching

When someone came to one of my derby league practices, I hoped they could let go of any preconceived notion about Roller Derby practice and what they thought about how it should look. This especially held true when someone had other derby experiences and thought we weren't doing drills because we weren't aware of them. Get ready for that.

We were structured with a sequential learning plan that doled out drills over time while correlating to skill level. Of course, everyone always has room in their toolbox (including me) and should always keep looking within to revise any overall vision. This guide will identify the skills needed (mental and physical) for each level of skater, beginners through the travel team.

WALK THE TALK...just sayin'.

Walking the talk is often easier said than done; as coaches, we need to keep reminding ourselves and each other to keep doing our best. People (particularly derby people) easily drift into the place of only being able to see their own experience; it can be challenging for humans to see a bigger picture beyond themselves.

A coach's success depends on having the ability to look at their own coaching style and behavior, conduct a personal assessment/reality check, and be willing to tweak their habits. We've all seen the coaches who thrive on intimidation and/or use their team to fill a void in their own lives or egos.

Coaches described below will show up with loud whistles and matching low self-esteem. These people abuse their authority, and their athletes perform and/or operate out of fear. A despotic coaching style feeds into an environment of negativity, control, and bullying. Some potentially great future athletes can be lost if the vibe of the practice is negative all the time or they don't understand their own value or possibilities.

On the flip side, there is a soft and gentle way that can be coddling, which doesn't do much to inspire or help athletes step up to find their strength. The middle ground is an obvious place to shoot for. Most important is knowing when to lean towards one end of the spectrum or the other.

Rookies can't be expected to behave like advanced skaters, and our job is to show them a way to replace self-doubt with self-confidence over a reasonable amount of time. Coaches need to be able to demonstrate skills during the entire practice and need to be able to do the fundamentals that are being taught to the skaters. This means getting onto the floor to demonstrate skills before and during practice.

If an injury prevents a coach from being able to demonstrate, they should have an assistant readily available to offer the visuals. A coach who has never personally mastered the skills they expect to teach should not be coaching.

Team performance and function are not very effective

if skaters feel powerless and have no say in their goals. A team's collective goal should be introduced so skaters have self-directed guidelines to follow. Think about a common goal for the team; let them work it out together, but stick to it.

Coaches

- Identify YOUR goals.
- Keep a strong and winning mindset.
- Display self-confidence.
- Overcome drama, adversity, and crap.
- Get a grip; gain control of negative thoughts.
- Use visualization and teach it as well.
- Employ stress management and relaxation techniques.

If a coach is fearful of new blood or the wrong fresh meat rocking the boat, they are probably afraid of the growth or challenges that they personally might need to face.

See derby drama. Talk to your skaters; don't ignore

anyone.

A coach needs to keep reminding themselves that they need to grow and improve as much as they expect their skaters to. It is critical for a coach to remain open to new experiences that will challenge their way of coaching or thinking. This can be humbling and difficult to do, but it really is an opportunity, not a problem.

• Use mistakes as an opportunity to change yourself; don't blame others for rocking the boat.

• Reinforce the good stuff and compliment a well-executed move.

• Silence doesn't convey that things were done right; it can easily be misinterpreted.

• Be aware of the communication process as you teach, i.e., tone, language, and non-verbal communication.

• Be willing to change things to keep the flow and let go of the plan when you need to.

• Maintain a consistent teaching point of view. A coach who loses hope loses motivation.

• Introduce the mental skills and talk about them.

- Help skaters find the obstacles and the way to get around them.

- Keep it simple.

- Be repetitive.

Remember

A skater's entire experience is influenced by what a coach does and can lead to changes that spread to other areas in life. Don't forget that what a coach says and does really matters. If you help people find the opportunity to change their lives, you contribute to their future, families, and communities.

Coaches Empower Their Skaters

If a skater feels powerless, they won't be in control of their goal-setting, and it will be much harder for them to act with intention. Teams must have guidelines and have a unified goal to experience the group efficacy to be champions. If a coach cannot follow this philosophy, it will be nearly impossible for the skaters to follow suit.

Don't Play Favorites

- Assume athletes don't know; repetition is a primary

tool for teaching.

- Don't talk about more than what is necessary.
- Be objective, with purpose. Talk about the situation, not the person.
- Be certain that assistant coaches teach the same principles and maintain the vibe.
- Connect with all team members, not just the best of them.
- Encourage feedback.
- Create an atmosphere that teaches and adheres to a high standard of behavior and execution. Help hold the athlete accountable.
- Remember that rookies are not ready to be All-Stars, but your All-Stars started as rookies.

Be an objective observer and problem solver. Instead of saying, "You are back blocking AGAIN," try an alternative such as "Are you looking at the holes that you can slide into?"

If there is someone that a coach doesn't like and won't talk to about, they should quit coaching. Effective coaches use mistakes as a vehicle for teaching rather than placing blame; it is much better to rcinforce a job well done. Awareness of communication, i.e. tone, timing, language, and non-verbal communication, is another aspect a coach should try to be aware of. It is possible to be direct without being rude. I like to tell my skaters something that I told my children. "It is ok to be angry, but not ok to be rude." Simple, right?

Maintaining a consistent teaching message is also good to remember. Waffling will confuse many skaters. A coach who loses hope in their skaters can damage motivation. It is good to introduce the factors involved in the mental aspect of performance and the obstacles in the way and help skaters find ways to get around them.

Group Focus

nowhereman photos Seattle WA

Team performance and function overall aren't effective if the skaters feel they are powerless and have no say in their own and the team's goals. Coaches should provide an opportunity to provide a team covenant and then stick to it. If a coach themselves can't adhere to the guidelines of a team covenant, the skaters won't have an opportunity to do so either.

By identifying a skater's personal goals at the beginning of each practice, it will eventually become apparent that each person's goals will only be obtained by working on the same skills as everyone else, thereby introducing group cohesion & goals.

This is all part of what is necessary to achieve a strengthening-bonding experience for skaters. This can be problem-solving with a skater or addressing derby drama.

We want to teach skaters to make decisions in the moment that will allow them to perform under stress and anxiety. Some of the best skaters at practice will fall apart when the spotlight is on them, and often, in competition, the meek ones jump out to surprise everyone.

It is a mistake to assume to know how someone will perform under stress. If skaters are trained from the beginning to take the focus off of themselves and aim it at the overall situation, it will help prepare them for future high-profile skating situations.

Teaching skaters from day one to keep their eyeballs off of the floor and train on someone else is a valuable tool. New skaters should look around and behind them while moving forward on their very first day on skates. A student's learning is influenced by the teacher's expectations, so never lose hope in a skater's ability to improve.

Practices

Start EACH PRACTICE by asking each skater what their personal goal is for the day.

They will most often say:

- Transitions
- Endurance
- Agility
- Crossovers
- Stopping
- Pack Work
- Whipping / Assists
- Starts
- Whatever

ALL of the listed items are achieved by the same things:

- Quad strength
- Core strength
- Weight transferstance

- Self-confidence awareness

Please remember this, I say again:

- Quad strength
- Core strength
- Weight transferstance
- Self-confidence awareness

After they can do all of the above confidently, they should do them even **lower and wider** and push themselves harder. *"Derby" drills at rookie practice should be in place only to make skaters feel familiar with what they expect to get out of practice.* In time, only advanced skaters will have a wide variety of drills.

Have beginners master the basics and build up the necessary mental and physical strength to make the decision to proceed as competitive skaters.

Your Beginners Should Learn

- Weight transfer to balance on each foot BEFORE WORMING or Weaving.

- To look behind while skating from day one, they'll need constant reminders to learn awareness of where their teammates are at.
- How to skate low(er) ALL of the time

They need constant emphasis to learn weight transfer to know where their center of gravity is BEFORE learning T-Stops or Transitions.

Warm Ups

Doing your stretching *after* warm-ups is a good practice rather than stretching when everyone is cold.

Skater Stance: demonstrate a strong skater stance, explaining from the waist down, they should ALWAYS reset to a strong position and from the waist up, they should be fluid and have a relaxed upper body, easily turning their heads and shoulders independently from their lower body.

- Engage the abdomen, quads, thighs, and butt muscles.
- Pelvic Tilt.

- Loose upper body.

Toe Stops Step

- Description - Demonstrate this in slow motion. 1- Low and wide. 2- Move butt over right skate. 3- Line up center of chest over knee, show that your shoulders and your body are a T. 4- Lift other foot. 5- Repeat on other side.

- Beginners - 1 toe stop on the ground as they learn to shift their weight from one leg to the other and back, returning to stance, repeating on the opposite side.

- Advanced - stepping on toe stops while transferring weight from one leg to other

Stepping / Sidestepping / Grapevine

We usually start our warm-ups with some balancing from one side to the other, squatting, moving feet, and then sidestepping. Advanced skaters can do this on their toe stops, but beginners should begin to be aware that their entire body weight will be shifting from being over one leg or the other. Keep reminding skaters to be:

- Lower
- Wider

Look around the room – Don't look at the floor

1" heel "pops"

Keeping stance and front wheels on the ground, "pop" heels / rear wheels off the ground, moving one inch right then left, and adding hips to exaggerate the transfer of weight.

1- Step 90. From a strong skater stance, have your skaters lift one skate off of the floor by pushing with the other foot, then do a one-quarter turn, landing with both toes pointing away from each other in a squat, knees pointing out. Then, back to the original position. Continue this with instruction to have the skater work even lower and wider, tightening their core and keeping their eyes off of the floor.

Repeat on the other side.

2- Step 180. Continue the above by adding one more step so they end up in a 180 from their original position. Advance skaters can do this in one hopping motion.

Repeat

Wall Turns

Keep reminding skaters to be strong, low and solid and to keep their EYES off of the floor. Beginners can do this along a wall as detailed below:

1 hand on the wall with arm outstretched to the side, then they open their stance to both toes pointing the opposite direction.

2 hands on the wall behind them / out to their sides, then complete the move by placing **one hand** on the wall. It is now the opposite hand from the one that they started with, and they are now facing the other direction.

Steps turnaround 360

Repeat the above drill with adding moves for a complete 360 in both directions.

- Low
- Wide
- Solid

Eyes on someone else

This is a good time to take this into some warm-ups to work on transitions. As your advanced skaters work on their transitions, either with the fundamentals of "opening and closing the door" or a hop in a reverse direction, your beginners can continue with the stepping motions in place or along the wall, as detailed below. Encourage your skaters to shift their weight to their strong leg BEFORE and AFTER they change directions. If their strong leg remains beneath them as they resume a solid skater stance, their rear leg can be behind them, and they can "land" in a "start" position, ready to race back to the track with toe stops on the ground.

Team your skaters up to take this to another level of working together:

Plow stops

Teaching the plow stop is one of the first stops, and warm-ups are a good time to review. In a skater stance, skaters slow and/or stop by bending their knees and sliding wheels outward with toes slightly pointed in. A good tip is to tell skaters to SKID their wheels and get

LOWER and WIDER.

Warm up notes

Emphasize "core" and skater stance — rigid / braced from the waist down and flexible upper body and shoulders from the waist up. Step, toe stop, weight transfer, side stepping, and 4 steps around in a 360. Break down transitions to work on proper mechanics of weight transfer, the opening of hips, and immediately dropping low to rigid skater stance to ending in a toe stop balance on both feet ready to start. Weaving from line to line with emphasis on lateral movements, toes to the line, eventually opening up a stance too wide and low with the forward toe pointing at t h e line and shoulders low for momentum (butt rudders). Skate while turning upper body to look at the far line (look at the outside line while looking over the left shoulder and the inside line while looking over the right shoulder).

Do Some Drills!

Knee falls / Tucking to falling small

Falling small is important for many reasons and we need to repeat this until skaters can naturally "tuck" into a small position when they feel themselves begin to fall. Teach skaters to slowly lower themselves to the ground from a solid stance while rolling to gently placing one knee beneath them just prior to the other knee following. Many new skaters tend to JUMP onto both knees, which can be injurious.

T-Stop (for intermediate to advanced skaters)

Beginners should first practice balancing on one leg prior to attempting their 5 stops. Until they can place their weight over one leg, their T-stops won't work or will be unsafe. The basic T-stip is rolling on one forward "strong" leg while the other foot is placed behind the rolling foot in the shape of a "T". Most importantly, teach skaters to "scoop" their ankle so the outside wheels are the strongest point against the floor. When skaters drag their inside wheels, they can easily break an ankle if they lose their balance or someone falls on the dragging foot.

Transition Drill

In walls of 3 or 4, skaters begin to roll while watching the skater furthest to the left (lead skater). When this skater begins to transition, the entire wall does the same, basing its movements in anticipation of what the lead skater is doing. After the lead skater does two transitions, the skater on the outside of the wall sprints (waterfalls behind the group) to be the lead for the next two transitions. Encourage the skaters to go as slow as they need to in order to have a precise and synchronized line. Once they get into their zone, you have walls of skaters transitioning, stopping, starting and sprinting in perfect unison. This drill is also a good way to see who works well together and who can base their movements on the actions of another skater.

Stride

Now, you can take your warm-ups onto the floor to have your skaters work on their stride. Encourage practice on crossovers and tilting shoulders towards the inside around the corner. A good way to teach skaters to look behind them is:

Have skaters place their right knuckles behind their backs on their left hip and their left knuckles touching the outside of their right knee, then tuck their heads to look over their right shoulder to look at the skater behind them. Repeat on the other side.

Buttrudders – Weave Toe to Line

Roll around the track with the emphasis on toes

pointing to the outside or inside line. For beginners, emphasize both toes and both shoulders to line skaters are zig-zagging around the track. Remind skaters (even new) to LOOK behind them as they change direction.

Advanced skaters - Add **WIDE** and **LOW** stance with the forward toe pointing to the line—*exaggerate shoulders and arms (armpit over the forward knee). Emphasize looking behind/over a shoulder with each change of direction most of the time.*

Pace lines and worming

Breaking into two pace lines with the slower on the inside is a good way to finish warm-ups. We have the back-to-front weaving (worming) through the pack, and for the faster pace line we add having multiple skaters worm. Once each skater weaves from the back of the pack to the front, then have the last two skates do this together with the one behind holding on as if in a truck & trailer or shopping cart, but BOTH skaters are skating. Then, we do the same with 3, 4, and 5 skaters with an emphasis on lateral weaving and creating spaces for each other. You can add the same drills for reverse worming from front to back. Adding multiple skaters makes it trickier, slower, and much to think about.

Go

Purpose

Agility, team building, reflexes, non-verbal communication, endurance, reflexes, and skating without thinking are harder workouts if the group is small and is working on transitions or knee falls. THIS DRILL CAN BE TAILORED TO FIT ALL SKILL LEVELS, and it is very fun.

Description

Skaters form a large circle or two, depending on the size of the group. First skater starts by pointing at someone while maintaining eye contact, saying "GO," and skating to take the spot of the person they pointed at. After a skater is pointed at, they should then identify someone else WITHIN TWO STEPS of leaving their place to move to THAT person's spot. Once there, they can transition to a start position, knee fall, plow or T-stop etc. This is a great drill for skaters to increase their skills at any level. It is a good one for working on starts, stops, transitions, plow stops, knee falls, side stepping, or whatever. This drill can be changed up and modified and is great for getting skaters to move without thinking. It is a harder workout if the group is small and is working on transitions, knee falls, and starts. *Beginning skaters should skate with an emphasis on stance and form. Advanced-level skaters should have 2-3 skaters in the middle at all times, with an emphasis on quickness in picking the next skater.*

Teaching Crossovers

- First have skaters practice balancing on one leg by bringing one knee up to the chest, roll & balance, then alternate legs.

- Next, move to balance on a forward leg with one leg extended behind.

- Then introduce, while they are balancing on their RIGHT leg with left foot extended to start, "pointing" their left foot to the wall to the right, toes behind the right shoulder. Roll while holding.

- Do the first steps above with only balancing on left foot with right knee to chest; roll and hold.

- Do the steps above with only balancing on the right leg with the left leg extended behind them and toes pointing over their right shoulder

- Start to emphasize "falling" from their knee to chest to their right foot on the floor and giving a push at the same time with the rear extended leg that is pointing over their right shoulder. Soon, they will be doing crossovers with both feet pushing.

Killer

Purpose

Getting skaters to look around at the whole floor as they skate—eye contact and pack awareness.

Description

The coach goes down the line and whispers to each skater that they are NOT the killer or that they ARE the killer (pick one). Skaters roll out and make eye contact with each other as they skate. The killer points across their body while making eye contact with someone when they think no one else is looking at them. The person who is pointed at falls small to the floor and then remains there doing crunches or pushups as an obstacle to the rest of the skaters.

The killer tries to kill everyone off without being identified. If someone knows who the killer is, they can identify them, and if they are correct, the round is over. If they are wrong, they must fall to the floor.

Multiple Skater Worm

Purpose

Agility, teamwork, endurance.

Description

A pace line of 5+ skaters weaves from the back of the line to the front individually. The first person grabs another person as they plow in front of the line. As soon as they do this, they communicate with each other for the next skater to start. After each skater goes once, the last two in the line go through together (both skating; this is not a truck and trailer or shopping cart). Work up to lines of four skaters working to pass the first one in line, immediately adjusting to work as a group in order to change quickly.

Waterfalls

Purpose

Communication and teamwork

Description

Walls of 3, 4, or 5. AFTER all skaters have eye contact and reset, the outside skater weaves behind a wall to the inside line. Emphasize skaters physically moving one another off of the line and also while in the wall. Demonstrate a firm grip/push/pull.

Wall Weaving

Purpose

Teamwork, waterfalls, pack work, skating without thinking as a group, group contact, using hands to move each other, and agility.

Description

In walls of 4, the inside person covers the line. Inside person (skater #1) circles to the right in front of the person next to them (skater #2). When they leave the line to circle, the wall weaves in to cover the line. Then the skater goes behind skater #2, back in front and does the same thing with skaters #2 and #3, then with skater #4. As soon as skater #1 returns to the line, the outside person (skater #4) weaves behind the line to do the same thing, circling #1, #2, #3, and then #4.

Fearlessness Drill

Purpose

Endurance, pacing and approaching a pack to fast feet and increase speed through holes without fear. Teamwork, pack awareness and ability to approach the back of a pack with speed.

Description

Group splits into two packs that maintain opposite distances as well as a set distance between each other. They COMMUNICATE with each other about where the jammer is and make certain that the holes are easy for the jammer to go through. One or two skaters break from the pack, pace around, and when they reach 5' behind the next pack, they increase fast feet at 100% output. Then, when they break through, they pace to the next pack to do the same thing. When they reach the third pack, they plow at the front of the pack. Likewise, other skaters go.

Wall Transitions

Purpose

Teamwork, awareness, speed, agility, skating without thought.

Description

In a wall of 4, the inside person begins to skate, then decides when to do a transition to a toe stop start position. The wall attempts to do the same thing at the same time, following that person's lead. They do it a 2nd time, then after the 3rd transition, the outside skater waterfalls behind the wall to take the inside position and does the same.

Beginning skaters should do this very slowly with an emphasis on doing it together and in proper form. Lead skater should have an awareness of waiting for slower skaters. Advanced skaters should do this with speed and several "start" steps.

Drunken Sailors

Purpose

Agility, balance, weight transfer, relaxing upper body.

Description

With a relaxed upper body and exaggerated arms for balance, skaters lean onto their left leg and take a step, crossing right foot in front and stepping onto it, then left foot over right. Continue for several laps around the track.

Double Knee Falls

Purpose

Teaching the proper way to fall to the knees and get back up safely.

Description

Demonstrate falling from one knee to two knees with the ability to turn in the opposite direction and how to return to the start position for quick pack re-entry.

Monkey Rolls

Purpose

To teach skaters that they can fall small at high speeds while controlling their bodies to fall small and use their gear for protection.

Description

From a double knee fall, have skaters drop to a crouching position with knee pads, elbow pads and wrist guards on the floor, then roll on the upper part of their backs with knees to the chest while pushing themselves with their arm for momentum. They should land back in the beginning position of crouching on the floor with all protective gear on the floor, then quickly back up to a skating/start position.

5-Step Fast Feet

Purpose

Fast feet, endurance, and pacing/conserving energy, learning to hop or gain momentum while going through the pack

Description

On the whistle, skaters take 5 steps. Beginning skaters "march" loudly; higher skill levels take 5 running steps if crossing over on the corners; on straightaway 5 jogging steps (as if wearing sneakers)

Corner Glides

Purpose

Endurance.

Description

Skaters stride normally, gaining momentum on the straightaway, and crouch as low as possible on the corners.

Straightaway One-Foot glides

Purpose

Agility, balance.

Description

Skaters gain momentum on the corners and do one-foot glides on straightaway, changing feet on each side.

Crossing the Gym

Purpose

Agility, balance, learning crossovers, learning fast feet.

Description

If you are in a large flat track area, have all skaters form a line across the back of the room. Starting at one corner, skaters should step across while moving forward to the opposite side to the center of the room, with the right foot crossing over left. When they reach the opposite side in the middle of the room, they should repeat to the other opposite corner with the right foot crossing over left, then skate to return to the line. Once the first skater is near the first point of the room before changing directions, the next skater can begin, and the line is in a continuous motion.

Sprint Pace

Purpose

Endurance.

Description

Have skaters stride at approximately 60% of output as if they were lapping the track as a jammer. On the whistle, have them sprint until the next whistle blow as they "pace." It is good to learn to pace themselves, as well as a good endurance drill. For variety, you can have skaters stride normally on the straightaway, and then when they are on the corners, they can squat as low as they can to coast around the corner and return to pushing normally on the next straightaway. Have skaters crossover on the corners, then balance on one foot onthe straightaway,

Pushing Partner

Purpose

Having skaters become accustomed to pushing, grabbing and using one another in the pack. Also good for pack awareness and timing.

Description

Have skaters with partners skating in walls of 2 close to the inside line. Have a few "jammers" circling around the outside of these skaters briskly. The inside of the pair then attempts to push their partner into a jammer with the right timing to have them either hit the jammer or get in front of them.

Relaxation & Visualization

Something to try if you have time prior to competition and/or at the end of practice:

Wind down a practice with a progressive relaxation technique and visualization after stretching. Have skaters lie on their backs and take a few controlled breaths into the count of 10 and all air completely out to the count of 10, then have them breathe normally. Then, lead them through relaxing their bodies step by step.

- Toes
- Calves and shins

- Thighs
- Pelvis
- Shoulders
- Spine
- Elbows,
- Hands and fingers
- Neck
- Face Throat

Have them be aware of how it feels to be completely relaxed and feel each part of their body hitting the floor. Ask them to notice each part of their skin feeling the air. Have them imagine they are on a beach and can feel the sun, hear the waves and seagulls, and smell the salt air. Then, have them visualize themselves skating strong and easily. Be creative.

Mental Toughness

(Includes adaptations from Lisa Brown - Courage to Win)

- Focus
- Confidence
- Aggression
- Team Building

Mental toughness is an acquired skill that all athletes must have. Since almost half of Roller Derby skaters have never previously participated in any sports, they might start rolling their eyes when you try to talk about this. Then, they will proceed to gossip about you. See derby drama.

Seriously, though, players who aren't willing to talk about this aspect of sport are most likely not going to progress beyond skating at an intermediate level. Their focus is on their personal experience and struggles with an inability to see beyond their personal agenda. It is good for the coach to attempt to discuss mental toughness with intermediate skaters (Intermediate = skills without confidence or confidence without skills).

Therefore, this information is for YOU, the coaches, to know, harbor, cultivate, expand, revise, and use while training your players who choose to become athletes by improving their bodies, minds and overall experience of being a team player.

The following exercises in this section are conceptual interpretations/adaptations of basic principles that are taught in most general sports psychology publications. Roller Derby is a prime target for mainstream athletic training.

Focus is the ability to choose what you pay attention to. In order to perform your best, you need to focus on the movements, thoughts and/or external cues that help you accomplish the task at hand. During the course of any given competition, you'll probably pay attention to a number of different movements, thoughts, and/or external cues. Take a look at the different levels of attention below and think about which levels you spend your most time in. Write down roughly how much time in a game or practice your attention or focus is at each level. Afterwards, ask yourself the following questions: "Is it effective for me? Would I prefer to be on a different level? How can I focus to shift my attention to another level?"

If you're not always paying attention to what you want to, don't worry. Focus is a skill that can be improved and mastered.

The Levels of Attention

(Adapted from Eberspacher, 1990)

- Myself and my task (movement, technical and external cues).
- The environment (the floor, opponents, spectators etc.)
- Comparison: Is _ suppose to be (I should be/I should have).
- Winning/Losing (It's almost over, we're going to win/lose).
- Consequences of winning/losing (if we win/lose).
- Question of meaning (What am I even doing

here?).

- Out of the game (completely unrelated subjects).

Think about how often your mind wanders when you are playing rather than coaching. How often do you realize that your mind is wandering? When you are coaching, do you know which of your players have wandering minds or when? The answer is ALL of them, most of the time. Does this happen more when you are speaking or when you are playing? Is there a way to tell?

One of my skaters once told me (as a favor) that I talk too much. The biggest challenge I have had to date as a coach is how to give the information I have to share without over-talking about it.

Skaters are at practice to skate, to learn drills and to improve. It is logical to believe this will happen from the physical challenge they experience at practice. What they don't always realize is that the best way to achieve excellence isn't only from what they believe derby practice should look like; there is a bigger picture that involves gaining information that we learn through sport.

Skaters who've not experienced a sport before have

no way of knowing what they don't know. I've mentioned elsewhere the topic of learning to stop being "nice" and apologizing for who we are. Even as coaches, we need to keep learning the best way to convey necessary information while holding onto who we are. Teach the skaters to rise up and unleash their power when the heat is on, regardless of how difficult that may be.

Composure - Managing Intensity - Attention & Focus

Our overall objectives are to find ways to impart knowledge, inspire players, and give them skills to take our sport to where they want to go with it. Finding the way IN is the challenge because it isn't about US; it is about how Players who've not experienced a sport before have no way of knowing what they don't know.

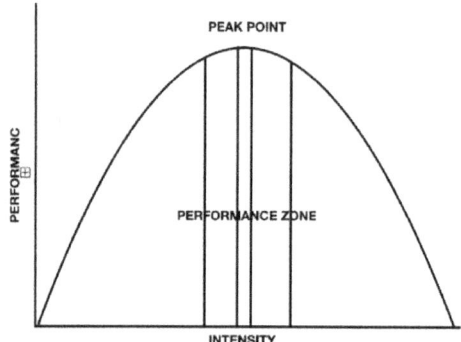

The optimal intensity for performance is:

- Related to TASK at hand.
- Level of intensity will vary between blocking and hitting on defense.
- Should be managed differently for varying phases of the game.
- Connected to attentional demands of the task.
- High intensity will narrow focus, and lower intensity broadens focus.
- General functions best at the same level that it is practiced.
- An INDIVIDUAL process (what works for YOU?).

- HIGH ENERGY and also retains a feeling of LOOSENESS.

Techniques for Managing Intensity

Method	Increasing	Decreasing
Breathing	**Short & Shallow Breaths** • Inhale / Exhale within 1 sec • Repeat for 5 seconds & stop	**Deep Belly Breathing** • Inhale 4 secs, exhale 8 secs • Repeat as needed
Muscle Tension	**Forcibly contract major muscles** • Contract legs, gluts and core muscles – hold for 5 secs • Take a short breath and then repeat	**Body Scanning** • Pay attention to your muscles one by one and consciously relax them, letting go of tension.
Music	Listen to music that pumps you up • Usually upbeat, loud / aggressive	Listen to chill music • Need I say more?

Often, fear is not even apparent to your skaters. They might be nervous, unfocused, jittery, or abrupt during a game, but they may not clearly know what it is about. If you can dig into what your skater is afraid of, you can help them overcome it. The first step is awareness, the second step is honesty and integrity (admitting it), and the third step is having the desire and commitment to overcome it.

There aren't any affirmations or positive self-talk methods that will replace hard work and determination to improve fitness level and ability.

Building Confidence

Athlete Malcom Gladwell said, "The people at the top don't just work harder or much harder, they work much, much harder."

Just because someone doesn't yet have skills, it doesn't mean they aren't CAPABLE of gaining the skills. What gets confusing in Roller Derby is that players can get lost in the glamour of the spotlight, even more than other sports. WHY? Often, players don't need much skill to get the admiration of others for playing Roller Derby. Just saying they play and having the willingness to take some knocks can bring about glory or add something that might be missing from their lives. What many players don't realize is that they will need to put in MUCH hard work in and out of practice, invest MUCH time with long-term commitment and devote their lives to physical training. This is the only way to be able to stand out as a top player.

Top athletes don't focus solely on being famous or rich or even winning. They focus on being their best every time they're on the track. Lisa Brown said that you need a weekly training program that has at least three categories: technical improvements, strategic improvements, and fitness improvements.

She also has something she calls the 10,000-hour rule for building confidence in sports. All extraordinary achievers put in a minimum of 10,000 hours developing their skills. Again, talent is a factor but not nearly as important as the work one is willing to put in to become the best at what they do. You can check her out at couragetowin.com.

Fake It Till You Make It

True or untrue? Actually, it is both. First of all, NO one knows what you are thinking or feeling. If you are afraid and don't show it, chances are you look better than you think you do.

Unfortunately, this can't last very long. As I've mentioned more than once, I like to say that intermediate skaters have either skill without confidence or confidence without skills. It is important to step out of the comfort zone, but it is as equally important to accept fears and weaknesses.

Confidence - Making the Choice

When we aren't worried about our performance, the physical output can be at a much higher level. This section talks about dependent and independent confidence. Both are used at different times for different purposes, and both are useful.

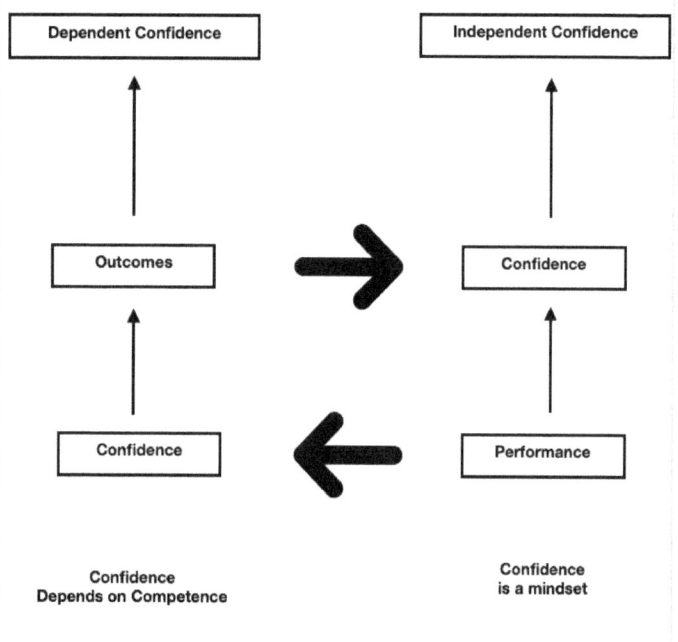

Building Independent Confidence

- Pay it forward. Right? Remember how it felt when you arrived? Take two minutes per practice to encourage someone new.

- Don't make comparisons to the past.
- Stay in the present, look forward to the next jam.
- Mistakes are part of the process, not something to avoid; they can be corrected after the game/bout and in practice.
- Independent confidence is connected to a stable and consistent skill; it doesn't change with the situation.
- Have "I know" statements & affirmations that are positive, personal, and memorable.
- Be fully committed to specific action/execution.

Aggression

Photo by Mike Wilson, Seattle WA - Bastardized by T.H. Flash

We all know about good aggression and bad aggression. I've always said that if someone could give me a group of skaters who are angry and know how to keep it zipped, I will show you an all-star team.

HOW do we get skaters who are upset, angry, emotional, and LOUD to channel that into physical output? Have you seen skaters who begin to lose their game when they become emotional? Of course, you have.

How do we get passive players to become more

aggressive? Few of us ever figure out how to de-program ourselves to learn to stop being nice or apologetic for being who we are.

Lisa Brown said that we can be nice AND aggressive (the good kind) if we quiet our minds, channel our determination, and just go for it.

Take Risks

If skaters are willing to step out of their comfort zone and take risks, not only is that confidence building, but it is also a way to take their heroes off of a pedestal.

Do you remember the first time you jumped over someone on a track? Did that bring about a fantastic feeling of self-confidence? Encourage skaters to step out to take risks when you know they are holding themselves back by their thoughts alone.

I had a skater who was super pumped (as a jammer) that she jumped through a fast moving wall for the first time. We had been working on our "fearlessness" drill and working on jumping through walls, beginning slowly and then increasing the speed. It kept her buzzing for the whole practice.

Keep repeating to your skaters to believe in

themselves, they need to be unstoppable, and that can't happen until they believe it.

Team Building

This is a very tricky part of being a coach. People need to be competitive, but it can go sideways if we put other skaters on a pedestal or become upset if they play better than us.

Here is one of the key issues with the structure of Roller Derby as it exists today. Everyone knows that in sports, you need to work your ass off to be a "starter" or to find a place on the roster. Most sports have divisions because they've been around long enough. Most leagues don't have skill divisions unless they've been around for a very long time. We don't have many opportunities to watch "C" league skaters compete with others of the same level. One answer to this would be to form as many teams as necessary to accommodate all skaters.

Think about how your league deals with training fresh meat and your policies regarding growth. How many "C" league skaters have the opportunity to gain the necessary skills to improve while skating in front of an audience to experience that kind of necessary pressure? How can a team skate with the philosophy that a team is only as strong as its weakest skater when they are threatened that they won't be able to play if others surpass them in skill level? The common answer to this is that it is the same in all sports. True, but most sports have more than one team or league in their area with ample participation available.

These are questions I can only address with my own league structure. *We need to work to the this sport into the mainstream.* If you are a skater, maybe you've gotten what you want, but please don't forget to further our sport and make it possible for people anywhere to be able to benefit from experiencing their own derby community.

Skill Levels

Beginners - Rookies - Fresh Meat

Frida Whipya
© 2012 donna kay

Beginning skater mental checklist

(H.A. Dorfman 2005 Coaching the Mental Game excerpts & adaptation)

- Begin to think about Identifying Goals
- Attempt to focus on self and others

Starting and Coaching a Roller Derby League

- Be responsible for own behavior; ASK for help
- Honesty
- Self Trust/Self Forgiveness
- Ability to accept coaching advice
- Keep an open mind
- Stay focused on the benefits: stay positive
- Be aware of adversity in the sport
- Be aware of your team
- Promise to try to do your best each time.

Roller Derby Rookie practice is about:

- Self Confidence
- Growth
- Opportunity
- Community
- Self Improvement
- Focus
- Determination
- Changing

- Learning
- Helping
- Mentoring
- Enjoyment
- Exercise
- Focus
- Intention
- Preparation

Beginning/Basics Specific Skills

No skating experience is necessary.

Overall Objectives

- Introduce the concept that a team is only as good as its weakest skater
- Balance, squats, rotation with an upper-body looking in 360
- Moving heels side to side off the floor in a derby stance
- Teach lifting feet to Open / Close the door in 2 steps, doing a 180 turn
- Derby stance while rolling
- Teamwork/communication are key
- Warming up and stretching
- A basic understanding of plow stops and T-stops
- Knee falls

- Pace line
- Truck and trailer
- Skater stance
- Stride with side pushes
- Low and Wide
- Shifting weight over lead leg/glides

Beginning Basics, Skill Specifics

In time, only advanced skaters should have a wide variety of drills. Have beginners master the basics and build up the necessary strength mentally and physically to make the decision to proceed as competitive skaters.

The most important part of teaching beginners is to teach them to start thinking about weight transfer and their center of gravity. Beginning to shift their weight over one or the other leg will get them ready for T-stops and intermediate skating. Coaches will probably know early on which skaters will not push themselves to make it through in the big picture, but I like to let that thought go with the hopethat they will surprise everyone.

There is nothing preventing a skater from public

competition or gaining strength other than the skaters themselves. Every skater should be given the tools to let go of self-doubt and gain self-confidence; again, it is their choice to take the toolsthat are offered or not.

Make sure beginners learn to weave, transition, look behind them, and skate low while learning to have an awareness of where their teammates are at.

Derby drills at rookie practice should be in place only

Photo by Gwen Etches, Seattle WA

to make skaters feel familiar with what they expect to get out of practice.

Intermediate Skaters

My personal definition of an intermediate skater is they have skills without confidence, or they have confidence without skills.

Additions to the mental skills checklist

(H.A. Dorfman 2005 Coaching the Mental Game excerpts & adaptation)

- Consistency of focus
- Responsibility to do what the situation requires
- Ability to cope effectively with adversity
- Gain awareness of opponents' presence and posturing
- Ability to do their best each time

Before introducing many "drills," you should make certain that skaters

- WANT to improve
- Can identify exactly why they are skating

- Can weave, shift their weight, maintain eye contact with other skaters
- Have confidence in their ability to focus on the MENTAL aspect of learning
- Skate powerfully, fast, and relaxed
- Mirror each other in walls of 4
- Transition
- Think fast
- Overcome self-doubt
- Weave horizontally in unison with another skater.

Have them strongly push and pull each other on and off lines, in waterfall drills and walls. Make sure skaters are always prepared to assist with holding arms out and behind them as a rule when they are not actually reaching out and looking behind them for an assist.

Remind them to always reset immediately to a strong stance after doing ANYTHING.

Intermediate Skaters should be able to skate in a proper stance and perform Crossovers, Plow Stop and T-Stop while looking behind them.

Overall Session Objectives

- Introduce the concept that a team is only as good as its weakest skater
- Introduce some team strategy
- Warming up and stretching
- 180-turn in 2 steps while rolling from forward to backwards skating (transition)
- A basic understanding of plow stops and t-stops, knee falls
- Double knee falls and return to skating within 2 seconds
- Pace line at increased speed and closer distance
- Worm through pace individually, then with 2, 3, and 4 skaters forward
- Reverse worm through pace line
- Truck and trailer with multiple people
- Skater Stance lower and wider
- Easy stride with side pushes
- Shifting weight over lead leg / glides easily on the

straightaway with each foot

- Walls with a minimum 1' skater at shoulder distance
- Side to side stepping away from wall
- Squat and coast through the entire straightaway and turn

Remember, Kindness is NOT a weakness. Discipline is not mean.

Overall Intermediate Skill Objectives

- Pace lines with speed and be able to touch the skater in front
- All stops, T, plow, and hockey
- Start drills
- Jammer drills
- Reverse direction skating
- Backwards skating
- Pack skating at increased speeds
- On and off skates endurance drills

- Worming at high speeds, reverse worming
- Sprinting
- Hip checks and shoulder checks
- Positional blocking scrimmages
- RESETTING with the team immediately after each drill.
- Able to coast, smooth striding in skater stance, easily perform crossovers, Plow Stop and T Stops

Roller Derby Advanced Practices should be about Roller Derby and skills training.

Advanced Skaters Overall Objectives

- IMPLEMENT actions with the concept that a team is only as good as its weakest skater
- Increase team strategies, waterfalls and pack skating
- Introduce Hockey stops
- 4-point fall, 180-degree turn fall, baseball slide
- Pace line with increased speed touching skater in

front

- Smooth stride, can run around corners
- Low and Wide, easy line-to-line weaving
- Walls of 4 shoulder to shoulder while touching neighbor's skates
- Transitions to backwards skating
- Squat and coast through the entire straightaway and turn
- Scrimmages with full-hitting
- Giving and receiving whips, inside/outside/hip
- Giving and receiving pushes

All-Star Skater Mental Checklist Additions

(H.A. Dorfman 2005 Coaching the Mental Game excerpts & adaptation)

- Confrontational attitude and posturing- warrior mind-eye contact
- Belief in the obligation to avoid intentionally injuring an opponent
- Aggressiveness under control
- Ability to contain emotion under stress
- Ability to channel negativity to physical output
- Relentlessness
- Intensity
- Extreme competitiveness
- Desire to train/gain top-notch physical fitness
- Belief that a team is only as good as its weakest player

- Desire to fairly and legally obliterate opponent
- Ability to skate without thought; action as the first response
- Pack awareness every moment on the track.

Leader List

(H.A. Dorfman 2005 *Coaching The Mental Game* Appendix A from workshops with staff of theOakland Athletics and Florida Marlins)

Is the coach an effective leader or a non-leader?

- The LEADER helps clean up; the other presides over the mess.
- The LEADER appeals to the best in each athlete, keeps his door open, is a problem solver, an advice giver, and a cheerleader. The other is invisible—gives orders to their staff and athletes and expects them to be carried out perfectly.
- The LEADER thinks of ways to make people more productive and more focused on team goals. The other things—personal status and how they look to others.

Starting and Coaching a Roller Derby League

- The LEADER is comfortable with people around him/her. The other is uncomfortable.

- The LEADER arrives early and stays late. The other is in late and leaves on time.

- The LEADER has the common touch. The other is strained with minorities or people different from them.

- The LEADER is a good listener. The other is a good talker.

- The LEADER is fair. The other is fair to those above them and uses those below them.

- The LEADER is decisive. The other is tentative.

- The LEADER is humble. The other is arrogant.

- The LEADER is tough—and confronts tough problems. The other is elusive— and avoids as many problems as possible.

- The LEADER is persistent. The other hangs in only when they have something personal at stake.

- The LEADER simplifies. The other complicates (making things look difficult).

- The LEADER is tolerant of open disagreement. The other is intolerant.

- The LEADER has strong convictions. The other looks to others for a philosophy rather than for suggestions.

- The LEADER does dog work when necessary. The other is above that.

- The LEADER starts with the trust of the people. The other trusts only words and statistics.

- The LEADER delegates responsibility. The other will do everything and everything and decide everything—OR.

- The LEADER takes their rightful responsibility. The other is glad to let others do everything.

- The LEADER wants anonymity for themselves and publicity for their team and athletes. The other wants the reverse.

- The LEADER often takes the blame. The other looks for a scapegoat.

- The LEADER gives credit to others. The other takes it for themselves—and complains about their lack of good players.

- The LEADER gives honest, frequent feedback to his athletes. The other has information flow one way—into their office.

- The LEADER

- The LEADER gives honest, frequent feedback to his athletes. The other has information flow one way—into their office.

- The LEADER knows when and how to discipline people. The other ducks unpleasant tasks and/or has poor timing and touch when addressing them.

- The LEADER goes where the trouble is to help. The other resents the trouble and wants it to disappear.

- The LEADER has respect for all people. The other has respect for those who make them look good or those they need to please.

- The LEADER is consistent and steady under pressure. The other improvises, equivocates, and passes the buck.

- The LEADER prefers eyeball-to-eyeball

communication. The other prefers messengers and meetings.

- The LEADER is straightforward. The other is tricky and manipulative.

- The LEADER is consistent and credible to the team. The other is unpredictable, often saying what they think they want to hear.

- The LEADER admits their own mistakes and assists the athletes when they admit theirs. The other never makes mistakes and blames those who do.

- The LEADER is open. The other is secretive.

- The LEADER avoids making promises they can't keep. The other indiscriminately promises much and delivers little.

- The LEADER is focused with great intensity on the team's values and objectives. The other is focused on themselves.

- The LEADER tells the athletes the team comes FIRST. The other may deliver the same message but sees themselves as Number One and acts accordingly.

- The LEADER sees mistakes as an opportunity and responsibility to teach. The other sees mistakes as punishable offenses.

- The LEADER maintains a high standard for the execution of tasks in practice and competition., while understanding that humans are imperfect. The other maintains unrealistic expectations and holds everyone accountable for perfection—except themselves.

- The LEADER has energy and enthusiasm. The other calls coaching "a job" and acts as if it's an ordeal.

- The LEADER is loyal to their athletes and staff. The other is loyal to themselves.

- The LEADER is positive and optimistic. The other is negative and pessimistic.

- The LEADER COMBINES and BALANCES COMPASSION and STRENGTH. The other has only one of those traits—or neither.

- And, still, the LEADER recognizes and trusts

their own individual way of doing all the things they have learned from experience are required to be effective and exceptional. The other has been used by experience rather than being one who has used it—by learning from it.

References

H.A.Dorfman, (2005) Coaching th*e Mental Game; Leadership, Philosophies and Strategies for Peak Performance in Sports—And Everyday Life*. Lanham, Mary-land, Taylor Trade Publishing.

Starting and Coaching a Roller Derby League

Forms

I've tried to make these forms as generic as possible by removing the names of myleagues, locations, cities, etc, so you can write them with your own information. For more information or links to the forms, kindly contact me: thehotflash56@gmail.com.

- Sample Policies and Procedure Sample Articles of Incorporation Sample Bylaws
- Skater Agreement Coaching Agreement Facility Agreement Press Release Handout
- Emergency Contact Form Sponsorship Welcome Letter Sponsor a Skater Contest Sponsorship Levels
- General Sponsor a Skater Info Sample Proposal
- Statement of Qualifications (for submitting a proposal)
- Memorandum of Agreement - City Parks Facility Skater Application and Waiver

- Skater Evaluation

Member Policy & Procedures

TABLE OF CONTENTS

1. Welcome
2. History
3. Changes in Policy
4. Skater definition
5. Probationary period
6. Equal Skating Opportunity
7. Affirmative Action
8. New Member Orientation
9. Member Records and Admin
10. Changes of Personal Data
11. Safety
12. Building Security
13. Personal Property
14. Skater Requiring Medical Attention
15. Visitors

16. Standards of Conduct
17. General Guidelines
18. Skater Agreement
19. Attendance
20. Practice Schedule
21. Harassment Policy
22. Sexual Harassment Policy
23. Violence
24. Ethical Standards
25. Dress Code
26. Use of Gear
27. Smoking Policy
28. Solicitations
29. Complaint Procedures
30. Corrective Procedure
31. Crisis Suspension
32. Transfer Policy
33. Outside Leagues
34. Return of Company Property
35. Skater Reviews

36. Training and Workshops

Introduction

Our league is on a mission to mainstream the sport of Roller Derby and to build a community designed for growth and inclusiveness. Our members range from people wanting exercise or a social network to top-notch athletes. There is a place here for all levels of participation, as well as continual opportunity to change your intention along the way. We believe that life is about helping one another through the pack, which is not limited to Roller Derby.

Here, you will find friends, health, resources, and opportunities for self-growth.

This is a guide for skaters and all members to help you make the most of your membership in our world.

Welcome

Welcome! We are happy to have you as a new member of our Community!

Our mission is to create accessibility to the sport of Roller Derby beginning at the community level by offering instruction, fitness, competition, a social outlet and athleticism in an environment that is positive, supportive, inclusive and strong.

History

We began in (CITY & STATE) in 20XX by (NAME), who, after having the opportunity to skate with (LEAGUE) Roller Girls and again with (CITY) banked track league (LEAGUE), saw a need for accessibility to the sport of Roller Derby for people wanting to participate in the sport but not necessarily have the time or resources to become involved in a private league.

March X 20XX (CITY) Roller Derby began by teaching adult and junior skaters through the (CITY) Parks and Recreation in the city's first Roller Derby classes. Later that same month (CITY), Roller Derby started at (LOCATION). Classes began at (NAME) College in the Winter of 20XX and still continue. (LEAGUE) is now training All-Star and Travel Team skaters to represent their region.

(LEAGUE) has grown to be a resource for other leagues across the world to form and utilize the (LEAGUE) branding and circuit of competition.

Changes in Policy

This manual supersedes all previous skater policies and procedures.

While every effort is made to keep the contents of this document current, we reserve the right to modify, suspend, or terminate any of the policies, procedures, and/or benefits described in the manual with or without prior notice to skaters.

Member Definition and Status

A skater of_____is a person who regularly or occasionally skates atany of our leagues as a skater, coach, NSO, referee or who participates as a volunteer or represents us in any way at any location.

This group will be held to the same standards of performance by upholding the league's philosophy of mentorship, athleticism, and inclusion.

Probationary Period for New Members

After passing minimum skills participation, skaters are eligible to scrimmage and must do so for the 3 months unless they are transferring in from another league. For skaters who were actively skating in their other league at games (bouts), this period is reduced to one month. We monitor and evaluate every new skater for the time requirements and then make a determination for team and league placement.

MEMBER POLICIES

Equal Skating Opportunity

We are an equal skating opportunity league. Minimum guidelines are provided to assess skill levels for skaters wishing to advance their skills to participate on a team. All skaters passing the criteria to become advanced skaters will have the opportunity to participate on a team.

Attendance requirements will only be in place 30 days prior to a scheduled game or competition if the skater wishes to compete.

Affirmative Action/Diversity

Our league is committed to affirmative actions that will build on the strengths of our current membership base and continually enhance the diversity of our organization. Our actions include, but are not limited to, the following:

- 100% Inclusion
- Instruction
- Competition

New Member Orientation

The formal welcoming process, or member orientation, may be conducted by a league representative, including an overview of the company.

Member Records and Administration

The task of handling member records and related administration functions at this league has been assigned to the administrative offices. Personnel files will be kept confidential at all times and include some or all of the following documents:

- Contact Information
- Emergency Information
- Skill Levels and League Affiliation.

All medical records, if any, will be kept in a separate confidential file.

Change of Personal Data

Any change in a member's name, address, telephone number, marital status, dependents, or insurance beneficiaries, or a change in the number of tax withholding exemptions, needs to be reported in writing without delay to our admin office.

Safety

The safety and health of our members is a priority. Our league makes every effort to comply with all safety requirements. Our safety rules and regulations are the following:

- Proper gear worn at all locations
- First aid equipment at all practices
- Emergency aid available at all events.
- USARS or other designated insurance is to be purchased by each member.

Each member is expected to obey safety rules and exercise caution and common sense in all work activities, league bouts and scrimmages.

Building Security

Each and every member must follow the building security rules and regulations listed here:

- All members at all locations and facilities must wear full gear at all times while on skates.

- Each facility must be properly to local and city fire codes with an emergency exit clearly posted.

Skaters, members, volunteers, or employees are not allowed on any league facility property after hours without prior authorization from their league coachand facility supervisor and/or staff.

Personal Property

Our administrative office does not have a lost and found. Skaters should contact their head coach or facility that tracks lost and found property for any missing items.

Members Requiring Medical Attention

Members should report all injuries and accidents immediately to their head coach and then follow these steps:

1. Contact emergency aid if necessary.
2. All members immediately cease drill activity and take a knee until a determination is made regarding the severity of the accident.
3. Apply ice, if needed, to injured skaters.

4. Health-related issues.

5. Any member who becomes aware of any health-related issue should notify their head coach of health status as soon as possible, and may need a doctor's permission to resume skating activity.

Visitors at League Practice

Most of our practices are at public facilities, and visitors are allowed in the practices. When inviting visitors, members should request that visitors maintain a low profile and request permission from the coach prior to taking any photos.

Standards of Conduct - See Below.

General Guidelines and Payments

All members are urged to become familiar with our rules and the ruleset for whatever entity our league has chosen to be an affiliate of. All skaters are expected to follow these rules and standards faithfully at all times. The initial fee for our skaters is $xxx, which can be applied towards the monthly fee of $xxx. If a skater wishes to continue on a drop-in basis, the drop-in fees thereafter are $xxx.

If a skater is placed onto a team, they become an active dues-paying member and all dues are required to be paid no later than the 5th of each month. Skaters may pay online, and a link can be found on all skater forms, which require a digital signature.

When a member leaves, they will give a 7 days' notice to avoid the following month's billing cycle.

* Dues are subject to change.

Attendance and Punctuality

We expect all coaches, volunteer coaches, and members to be ready to begin at the beginning of scheduled practice and to reasonably complete their cooldowns and exit by the end of scheduled facility hours.

Practice Schedule

If a member is scheduled for participation in a game or competition, they must comply with that league's mandatory practice for 30 days beforehand. Other than that, we do not require attendance to keep a place on a team. If a member is absent for 1 month without contacting their head coach or league admin, it will be assumed that that skater does not wish to continue with their team.

Harassment Policy

Our league does not tolerate harassment. Bullying and harassment can take many forms. It may be, but is not limited to, words, signs, offensive jokes, cartoons, pictures, posters, e-mail jokes or statements, pranks, intimidation, physical assaults or contact, or violence. ALL of our facilities are conducted with good sportsmanship as a priority, and it should be known to all league participants that all participating facilities are considered to be "bully-free" zones.

Our league is committed to providing skaters with an environment free fromintimidation, threat, offense and humiliation. To provide a safe environment, we must be free from all types of harassment or any behavior that is unwanted by another person.

To meet this commitment, all members will be guided by this policy.

Harassment, bullying and vilification are not and will not be tolerated underany circumstances.

Harassment is a form of discrimination. Harassment includes any behavior,whether verbal, non-verbal or written, that is unwelcome, uninvited or unreciprocated and that a reasonable person, having regard to allcircumstances, would understand as being offensive, humiliating or intimidating. It is against the law if the discriminatory behavior is based on a person's race or color; national or ethnic origin; sex, pregnancy or marital status; gender history;age; disability, impairment or illness (including HIV/AIDS status); religious or political conviction; sexual preference; and/or that of any of their friends orassociates.

Bullying refers to the repeated less-favorable treatment of one person by another or others within our league that may be considered unreasonable and inappropriate sporting or social conduct, either in person or online. Bullying is behavior that intimidates, degrades or humiliates. This may include physicalabuse, mobbing, verbal abuse (such as taunting, yelling or screaming, name calling and offensive language), psychological harassment, excluding or isolating someone, assigning someone meaningless and irrelevant tasks or impossible tasks, etc.

Vilification is the incitement of hatred, serious contempt or severe ridicule of aperson or group of people on the grounds of an attribute such as race, sexual orientation and so forth. Vilification is unlawful.

Note: Harassment, bullying and vilification need not be verbal and need not be done in the direct presence of the target to be deemed to have occurred. Methods can include emails and onlinepostings, phone calls and SMS text messages, pictures, graffiti, gestures,exclusion of a person, interfering with a person's equipment or property, gossiping or spreading rumors, etc. Members should feel confident to complain about harassment, bullying and vilification without any reservations. No individualwill be victimized for speaking out about or against harassment in our community.All cases will be taken seriously and investigated, and incidents will be dealt with quickly, fairly, impartially, and confidentially. If serious enough, legal action may be taken against an individual who is found to have harassed or vilified another person.

Our league has a procedure for members to notify their head coach of their concerns. *See #29

The Head coach must deal with the matter in accordance with league policies.

Procedure and a complainant. A respondent or other involved party is always afforded their right to appeal in accordance with the procedure.

Our league takes harassment matters seriously, and those found in violation of the Harassment Policy may face disciplinary action or expulsion. We may take similarly strong action in the case of false accusations. In general, members should work towards portraying the club in a positive light.

Be yourself, be unique, but please be mindful that your actions when engaged in Roller Derby or an affiliated event will reflect on the Roller Derby community as a whole. As stated in the Mission Statement, our aim is to promote the sport over the spectacle and to be portrayed to the public as doing such. Any member found violating this Code of Conduct will have their membership reviewed by the administrative board, and action, such as a formal warning or expulsion without refund of dues paid, may be taken.

Sexual Harassment Policy

Our league does not tolerate sexual harassment. Sexual harassment may include unwelcome sexual advances, requests for sexual favors, or other unwelcome verbal or physical contact of a sexual nature when such conduct creates an offensive, hostile, and intimidating skating environment and prevents an individual from having the experience that we wish to provide.

Violence in the Community

We have adopted a policy prohibiting violence. Consistent with this policy, acts or threats of physical violence, including intimidation, harassment, and/or coercion, which involve or affect our league or which occur on our facility property, will not be tolerated.

Ethical Standards

Our league insists on the highest ethical standards in conducting its business and training. Doing the right thing and acting with integrity are the two driving forces behind our success plan. When faced with ethical issues, skaters, coaches, volunteers, and leaders are expected to make the right professional decisions that are consistent with our principles and standards.

Dress Code

Be an individual, be yourself, and it is policy that you do not wear dangling jewelry of any type during scrimmages or games. If you have large jewelry (i.e., hoops) that cannot be removed, please TAPE to your skin while participating as amember.

Use of Equipment

All skaters must provide their own skating gear for participation in this league. Scholarships are available for anyone who needs help in obtaining proper equipment.

Smoking Policy

Smoking of any kind is prohibited inside any skating facility. Smoking may take place only in designated smoking areas outside of facilities and is strongly discouraged by any coaches while in the presence of skaters, as they are viewed as mentors and leaders.

It is the policy of our league that any skating facility be free of illicit drugs and alcoholic beverages and free of their use. An exception to alcohol usage is at events where use is permitted, and if participants are on skates at these events, any intake of alcohol is prohibited. In addition to damage to respiratory and immune systems, malnutrition, seizures, loss of brain function, liver damage, and kidney damage, the abuse of drugs and alcohol has been proven to impair the coordination, reaction time, emotional stability, and judgment of the user. This could have tragic consequences where demanding or stressful situations call for quick and sound decisions to be made.

Solicitations and Distributions

Solicitation for our league is not permitted unless it is for seeking sponsorship for the league and all materials have prior approval by the head coach and the administrative team. Members are encouraged to share non-company literaturein facilities at any time for worthy causes or for skating-related purposes.

Complaint Procedure

Members who have a league-related issue, question, or complaint should first discuss it with their head coach or supervisor. If the issue cannot be resolved at this level, we encourage members and coaches to contact the administration. Members who observe, learn of, or, in good faith, suspect a violation of the Standards of Conduct (*see #16) should immediately report the violation in accordance with the following procedures:

1. Call it when you see it
2. Attempt to resolve between involved parties

3. Fill out the request for facilitation form

As a community member, under NO circumstances should a personal grievance or complaint be posted on any public internet group or forum. Please contact your coach for personal guidance on any issue or dispute needing resolution.

Corrective Procedure

Unacceptable behavior that does not lead to immediate suspension may be dealt with in any of the following manners: (a) Oral Reminder, (b) Written Warning, (c) Suspension.

Crisis Suspension

A member who commits any serious violation of our policies, at minimum, will be suspended without notice, pending an investigation of the situation. Following the investigation, the member may be terminated without any previous disciplinary action having been taken.

Transfer Policy

Our league recognizes that a desire for growth and other needs may lead a member to request a transfer to another position or location. A member will always be eligible for transfer to another affiliated league at the end of that year's skating season.

Outside Leagues

Members may skate with an outside skating group with a customer or competitor of our league and may do so on their own if it does not compete or interferes in any way with the sales of products or services that we provide to our skaters and written approval is given by the other league.

Return of Company Property

Any borrowed skates or gear that is loaned to skaters must be returned at the time of exit. Skaters will be responsible for any lost or damaged items.

Skater Reviews

We want to help skaters to succeed in their jobs and to grow. In an effort to support this growth and success, we have a skater self-evaluation form that the skater is expected to use, and skills must be initialed by a coach for advancement in their skill category.

Scholarship Assistance

We will review any requests for assistance from skaters who may not be able to afford monthly dues or insurance. Please contact your head coach for details or look at the forum for forms and applications.

Training and Workshops

We will be holding various training programs and workshops that all members willbe invited to attend. Stay tuned to our calendar for updates.

Sample Articles of Incorporation for Non-Profit

ARTICLES OF INCORPORATION OF (name of organization).

I

The name of this corporation is ____.

II

This organization is a nonprofit public benefit corporation and is not organized for the private gain of any person. It is organized under the Nonprofit Public Benefit Corporation.

Law for charitable purposes.

The Specific purposes for which this corporation is organized include, but are not limited to: [the preservation and management of parkland and delivery of programs for scientific, historic, educational, ecological, recreational, agricultural, scenic or open space opportunities.

III

The name and address in the State of [] of this Corporation's initial agent for service of process is:

Name:

Address:

COMMENT: Section III indicates to the Secretary of State and other interested parties the name of the person to whom legal documents must be sent. Theinitial agent is usually one of the initial directors of the corporation. If the corporation has established a principal office, this address should be listed as theagent's address. Otherwise, the agent's home address is acceptable.

IV

The corporation is organized and operated exclusively for charitable purposes within the meaning of Section 501(c)(3) of the Internal Revenue Code.

Notwithstanding any other provision of these Articles, the corporation shall not carry on any other activities not permitted to be carried on (1) by a corporation exempt from federal income tax under Section 501 (c)(3) of the Internal Revenue Code or (2) by a corporation contributions to which are deductible under Section 170(c)(2) of said Code, or the corresponding provisions of any future statute of the United States.

No substantial part of the activities of this corporation shall consist of carrying on propaganda or otherwise attempting to influence legislation, nor shall the corporation participate or intervene in any political campaign (including the publishing or distribution of statements) on behalf of any candidate for public office.

V

The names and addresses and office held of the persons designated to act asthe initial Board of Directors of this corporation are: [List their names and addresses. Most states require a minimum of three Board Members/Officers for incorporation purposes.]

VI

The property of this Corporation is irrevocably dedicated to charitable purposes, and no part of the net income or assets of the corporation shall ever inure to the benefit of any director, trustee, member or officer of this corporation or to any private person.

Upon the dissolution or winding up of the corporation, any assets remaining after payment of, or provision for payment of, all debts and liabilities shall be distributed to a governmental entity described in Section 170(b)(1) (A)(v) of the Internal Revenue Code, or to a nonprofit fund, foundation, or corporation which is organized and operated exclusively for charitable purposes, which has established its tax-exempt status under Section 501(c)(3) of the Internal Revenue Code, and which is qualified to receive "qualified conservation contributions" within the meaning of Section 170(h) of said Code, or the corresponding provisions of any future statute of the United States.

In the event of a liquidation of this corporation, all corporate assets shall be disposed of in such a manner as may be directed by decree of the superior court for the county in which the corporation has its principal office, on petition, therefore, by the Attorney General of by any person concerned in the dissolution, in a proceeding to which the Attorney General is a party.

IN WITNESS WHEREOF, the undersigned, being the Incorporators of [name of nonprofit] and the initial directors named in these Articles of Incorporation on _____, 20__.

Incorporators Signature

_____

[typed name], Incorporator

[Signature]

_____ _____

[typed name], Incorporator

[Signature]

Directors Signature

_____

[typed name], Director

[Signature]

_____

[typed name], Director

[Signature]

Sample Articles of Incorporation

COMMENT

The minimum actual number of Incorporators and the number of Directors depends on your state's non-profit incorporation requirements that can be obtained from the Secretary of State or known to law offices or published in non-profit guidebooks. It is advisable to have at least three directors.

Also note that if the initial directors are named in the Articles of Incorporation, it is not necessary to have incorporators. However, having both incorporators and initial directors may be advisable if the nonprofit wishes to demonstrate broad community support.

Remember that any incorporators and all named directors must sign the Articles of Incorporation, as provided for above, and must also acknowledge having signed the Articles. This acknowledgement must be a separate form from the body of the instrument (see sample declaration below).

DECLARATION

We are the persons whose names are subscribed below. We collectively are allof the incorporators of _____[name of nonprofit}_____and all of the initialdirectors named in the Articles of Incorporation, and we have executed these Articles of Incorporation. The foregoing Articles of Incorporation are our act and deed, joint and severally.

Donna Kay

Executed on _____, 20__,

at _____.

[city and state]

We, and each of us, declare that the foregoing is true and correct.

_____ _____

[signature]

_____

[typed name], Incorporator

_____ _____

[signature]

_____

[typed name], Incorporator

_____ _____

[signature]

_____

[typed name], Director [signature]

Sample Bylaws for A Non-Profit

*Please be advised that the use of this and other generic templates can lead to costly legal implications in the future. This and any other sample or template document is for informational and planning purposes only and should not be filed with your state without proper legal counsel and review.

Sample Bylaws Non-Profit Corporation of

_____

LEAGUE NAME

ARTICLE I. NAME

The name of the corporation is the league name, hereinafter called the "Corporation."

ARTICLE II. PURPOSES

The Corporation is organized for the following purposes:

Section 1. PURPOSE

Section 2. PURPOSE

Section 3. PURPOSE

Section 4. PURPOSE

Section 5. PURPOSE

Lessing the burden of government through donations to other nonprofit funds, foundations, or corporations that are established as tax-exempt under Section 501(c)3 of the Internal Revenue Code.

ARTICLE III. MEMBERSHIP AND DUES

Section 1. Eligibility.

There shall be the following classes of individual membership ("Members"):

a. League Name. The League Name class of membership shall be granted subject to completion of all requirements set forth in the Corporation'sMembership handbook and

b. New Skaters. The New Skaters class membership shall be granted after completion and receipt of a membership application and current payment of dues.

Section 2. Voting Rights.

Only the (Your League) class of membership shall

have corporate voting rights.

Section 3. Resignation and Removal.

Any Member shall resign by filing a written resignation with the Secretary. The Board of Directors, by affirmative vote of two-thirds of all members of the Board, may suspend, expel, or terminate an individual member after a formal hearing according to the procedures contained in the Corporation's Membership Handbook.

Section 4. Dues.

Dues for Members shall be established by the Board of Directors.

Section 5. Committee Service.

Each Member shall serve on at least one standing committee.

ARTICLE IV. OFFICERS, EMPLOYEES, AND AGENTS

Section 1. Officers.

The Officers of the Corporation shall be a President, Vice-President, Secretary, and Treasurer ("Officers"), and such other officers at the Board of Directors may from time to time elect. One or more offices may be held by the same person, except the offices of President and Secretary.

Section 2. Duties of Officers.

Subject to the continuing authority of the Board of Directors, the officers of the Corporation have the duties and responsibilities assigned to them by the Boardof Directors from time to time, which, unless otherwise determined by the Board, will include the following:

2.1. President. The President shall preside at all meetings and shall be ex officio Chairman of the Board of Directors, and shall perform such other duties as are incident to the office or are properly required of her by the Board of Directors.

2.2. Vice-President. The Vice-President shall assist the President in the discharge of her duties, preside in her absence, serve on the Board of Directors and perform such other duties as may be assigned to her by the President or Board of Directors.

2.3. Secretary. The Secretary shall keep a full and complete record of the proceedings of all meetings and shall preserve all documents, reports, and communications connected with the business of the Corporation, send out all notices, compile the records for Bouts, and perform such other duties as usually pertain to the office. She shall also serve on the Board of Directors and perform such other duties as may be assigned to her by the President or the Board of Directors.

2.4. Treasurer. The Treasurer shall collect and receive all monies, keep a correct amount thereof, and deposit same in the name of the Corporation in such bank as may be approved by the Board of Directors. She shall manage the Corporation's taxes, including making any elections or filings required by the Corporation. She shall also serve on the Board of Directors and perform such other duties as may be assigned to her by the President or the Board of Directors.

Section 3. Election.

Each year, Officers shall be elected by majority vote at the Annual Meeting, by a quorum of Your League present. In case a vacancy shall occur in any officer position, the vacancy shall be filled by the Board of Directors, and the person chosen to fill such vacancy shall hold office until the next Annual Meeting atwhich the election of Officers is in the regular order of business.

Section 4. Removal.

Any Officer elected or appointed may be removed by the Board of Directors whenever in their judgment the best interests of the Corporation would be served thereby.

Section 5. Other Agents and Employees.

The Board of Directors may, from time to time, appoint such agents and employees as it shall deem necessary, each of whom shall hold office at the pleasure of the Board of Directors, and shall have such authority, perform such duties and receive such reasonable compensation, if any, as the Board of Directors may from time to time determine. The Board of Directors is authorized to delegate the authority and duties of any officer to any agent or employee of theCorporation as the business of the Corporation may require. All agents and employees shall hold their respective positions at the pleasure of the Board of Directors. They may be removed from office or discharged at any time with or without cause, provided that removal without cause shall not prejudice the contract rights, if any, of such agent or employee.

ARTICLE V. BOARD OF DIRECTORS

Section 1. Composition.

The Board of Directors shall be composed of the President, the Vice-President, the Secretary, the Treasurer, and up to seven additional individuals ("Directors-at-Large"). to the Director at her e-mail address as it appears on the record of the Board of Directors.

Section 2. Voting.

Every Director present, when a motion is under consideration, shall vote thereon unless excused. Voting by proxy shall be allowed and proxies shall be in writing and signed, but need not be sealed, witnessed, or acknowledged, and shall be filed with the Secretary at or before the meeting. Voting by proxy through e-mail shall be allowed by putting "vote" in the subject line, setting out the specifics of the vote in the message, and e- mailing to the Secretary at or before the meeting.

Section 9. Board of Directors Vacancy.

In case a vacancy shall occur in the Board of Directors, the vacancy shall befilled by the Board of

Directors, and the person chosen to fill such vacancy shall hold office until the next Annual Meeting at which the election of Directors is inthe regular order of business.

Section 10. Conflict of Interest.

Subject to the limitations in State Statute, any contract or other transaction between the Corporation and any one (1) or more of the Directors, or between the Corporation and any organization that involves one or more of the Directors as party or interested person, will be valid for all purposes, notwithstanding the presence of such Director or Directors at the meeting of the Board that actsupon, or in reference to, such contract or transaction, and notwithstanding such Director's or Directors' participation in such action, if the fact of such interest and all material facts of the transaction and the Directors interest are first fully disclosed to the Board of Directors at such meeting and the Board at suchmeeting nevertheless authorizes, approves, and ratifies such contract or transaction by vote of a majority of disinterested Directors upon a finding that the transaction is not unfair to the Corporation. Any interested Director or Directors will be counted in calculating whether a quorum is present, but will not be counted in calculating the majority necessary to carry such a vote. A Director is not considered an "interested" Director with respect to a matter involving anInstitution or its Institutional Affiliates merely because such Director is affiliated with the Institution.

ARTICLE VI. MEETINGS OF MEMBERS

Section 1. Time and Place of Regular Meetings.

There shall be an Annual Meeting of the Corporation to be held in the County [Location] in January, February, or March of each year. At the Annual Meeting, the members shall elect Directors-at-Large and Officers, receive reports on the activities of the Corporation, and determine the direction of the Corporation for the coming year.

Section 2. Special Meetings Convened.

Special meetings of the Corporation may be called at the request of the President or the written request of ten members.

Section 3. Notice of Annual Meeting.

a. At least thirty days prior to the Annual Meeting, the Secretary shall notify all Members of the slate of

Officers and Directors-at-Large up for reelection.

All Members can nominate a candidate to the slate of nominees, by notifying the Secretary of their nomination, at least two weeks prior to the Annual Meeting.

b. Notice of the Annual Meeting of members shall be in writing, stating theagenda, the place, date, and hour of the meeting.

c. Notice shall include the slate of nominees being considered for each position.

d. Notice shall be given, by e-mail or by mail, to each Member entitled to vote at such meeting and each Director-at-Large. If the notice is given by email or first class mail, it shall be given not less than ten nor more than fourteen days before the date of the meeting. Notice is given when deposited in the United States mail, with postage thereon prepaid, directed to the Member or Director-at-Large at her email address as it appears on the record of the Corporation.

Section 4. Notice of Special Meetings.

Notice of all special meetings of Members shall state the purpose or purposes for which the meeting is called.

Notice of any meetings shall be given, by e-mail or by mail, to each Your League. If the notice is given by e-mail or first class mail, it shall be given not less than three nor more than 30 days before the date of the meeting. Notice is given when deposited in the United States mail, with postage thereon prepaid, directed to Your League at the address as it appears on the record of the Corporation, or emailed to (Your League) at her e-mail address as it appears on the record of the Corporation.

Section 5. Minutes.

The minutes of the Annual Meeting or of any special meeting of the Corporation shall be read and approved at the next succeeding meeting of the Board of Directors.

Section 6. Voting.

Every Your League present, when a motion is under consideration, shall vote thereon unless excused. Voting by proxy shall be allowed, and proxies shall be in writing and signed, but need not be sealed, witnessed, or acknowledged, and shall be filed with the Secretary at or before the meeting. Voting by proxy through e-mail shall be allowed by putting "vote" in the subject line, setting out thespecifics of the vote in the message, and emailing to the Secretary at or before the meeting.

ARTICLE VII. COMMITTEES

Section 1. Standing Committees.

There shall be five (5) standing committees:

a. Public Relations. The Public Relations Committee is responsible for, but not limited to, media, publicity, community outreach, service, hospitality, and organizing community work events for the Corporation.

b. Fundraising. The Fundraising Committee is responsible for, but not limited to, obtaining sponsorship, advertising, grants, and merchandise.

c. Rules and Regulations. The Rules and Regulations Committee is responsible for, but not limited to, all Insurance issues, Inter-league relations, (Your association) rules and regulations, and all issues concerning referees.

d. Events. The Events Committee is responsible for, but not limited to, working with other committees for advertising and sponsorship, ticket sales, setup and takedown of the event, organizing volunteers, merchandise, and vendors, maintaining contact with the event facility, and maintaining team contact.

e. New Recruit. The New Recruit Committee is responsible for, but not limited to, determining the practice schedule for New Skaters, recruitment opportunities, the New Skater program, and requirements for becoming a Your League.

Section 2. Appointments.

Members of all standing committees shall be appointed by the Officers for a term of one year. Committee chairpersons shall be elected by the majority vote of the respective committee members.

Section 3. Special Committees.

The Board of Directors may, by resolution adopted by a majority of the Directors, establish Special Committees. The Board may make such provisions for appointment of the chair of such committees; establish such procedures to govern their activities, and delegate thereto such authority as may be necessary or desirable for the efficient management of the property, affairs, business, and activities of the Corporation.

a. **Grievance Committee**. The Board of Directors shall establish a Grievance Committee. The Grievance Committee shall establish due process to receive, hear and decide grievances. The grievance procedure shall be published in the Membership Handbook. The Grievance Committee shall follow the grievance procedure to report individual grievances, membership suspensions, termination, and removal issues to the Board of Directors, along with their recommendations.

b. **Finance Committee.** The Board of Directors shall establish a Finance Committee. The Treasurer is the chair of the Finance Committee, which includes three other Board Members. The Finance Committee is responsible for, but not limited to, developing and reviewing fiscal procedures and developing long-range financial plans for the Corporation. The Finance Committee shall assist the Treasurer in managing the Corporation's taxes and submitting the annual report, pursuant to Article IX, Section 1, below.

ARTICLE VIII. QUORUM

Two-thirds of the Your League shall constitute a quorum at any meeting of the Corporation. A majority of the Directors shall constitute a quorum at any meeting of the Board of Directors.

ARTICLE IX. REPORTS

Section 1. State Law Requirements.

The Treasurer shall present at the Annual Meeting a report, in accordance with the State Statute, verified by the President and Secretary or by a majority of the Directors, or certified by an independent public or certified public accountant or a firm of such accountants selected by the Board of Directors, containing the following information:

a. The assets and liabilities of the Corporation as of the end of a 12-month fiscal period termination not more than six months prior to such meeting.

b. The principal changes in assets and liabilities during the year immediately preceding the date of the report.

c. The revenue or receipts of the Corporation for the next year immediately preceding the date of the report.

d. The expenses or disbursements of the Corporation during the year immediately preceding the date of the report.

e. Any assets held by the Corporation in trust for, or with a direction to apply the same to, any specific purpose, and the use made of such assets and of the income thereof.

f. The number of members of the Corporation as of the date of the report, together with a statement of increase or decrease in such number during the year immediately preceding the date of the report, and a statement of the place where the names and places of residence of the current members may be found. The report shall be filed with the records of the Corporation and a copy thereof shall be entered in the minutes of the Annual Meeting of members.

Section 2. Committee Reports.

Every Officer, every Standing Committee, and Special Committees shall present reports to the Board of Directors and the Corporation at its Annual Meeting as the Board of Directors shall direct.

Section 3. Submission to Directors.

No report shall be presented to the Corporation at its Annual Meeting which has not been previously submitted to the Board of Directors. The Board may advise changes or demand additional information to be formulated in the report before it is presented to the Corporation.

ARTICLE X. PROCEDURE

Roberts Rules of Order, as last revised, shall govern

the proceedings of all meetings of the Corporation and of the Board of Directors.

ARTICLE XI. AMENDMENTS

Section 1. Procedure.

These Bylaws may be amended by vote of the majority of the Board of Directors present at an Annual Meeting or at any special meeting duly called for that purpose, provided that notices of such proposed amendments shall be mailed at least ten days prior to the day for which the meeting is called. Proposed amendments shall be submitted in writing to the Secretary at least 30 days before the date of the Annual Meeting or the special meeting.

Section 2. Compliance.

Any amendment to the Bylaws effecting a change in the number of directors, membership voting rights, or quorum shall conform to the provisions of the Nonprofit Corporation act of the State of _____.

Dated this_____day of, 20_____ _____

Name of member

Position Phone #

Email

Donna Kay

(repeat for each Board Member/Officer)

Skater & Volunteer Agreement

I understand that there is a zero (0) tolerance policy for negative remarks/comments regarding any Roller Derby league, team or organization. Making any such remarks is cause for suspension or dismissal.

I understand that if I should become an All-Star or travel team skater, I will agree to mentor other skaters and that my behavior should be positive and encouraging atall times. As a skater and/or mentor, I agree that I will not utilize exercise as punishment, nor will I resort to using language that is shaming, humiliating or rude.

I understand that our members encourage their peers to surpass them in skill level and do their best to remember that any team is only as good as its weakest skater.

I understand that compassion, tolerance, and communication are of the utmost importance for excellence. I understand that if I need help, I will ask for it, and I will not automatically assume that any strong skater has a superior attitude that is worthy of resentment.

I understand that even individuals who have weaker skills than me or my team are still important as members of our Community, and I will do my best to acknowledge their progress and answer their questions.

I understand that this is a Roller Derby league that will offer competitive teams with varying agendas and skills, and I must pass a skills test and assessment prior to moving to a new level or being placed onto a team.

I understand that once placed on a team, I am expected to play through to the end of that team's season. Travel Team's season is considered to end after that year's Regional/National tournament. If I leave my team for another local league during our skating season, the opportunity to return to our league will be subject to board approval on a case-by-case basis.

I understand that kindness is not weakness and discipline is not mean.

SKATER NAME

SKATER SIGNATURE

Starting and Coaching a Roller Derby League

DATE

Coaching Agreement

Letter of Agreement - Coaches:

This letter constitutes a contract between (Your League) league owner and _____ Head Coach (H.C), dated_____, 20__.

It is agreed that H.C. will lead league practices for the facility located at _____.

H.C. will show up on time to each practice and agrees to utilize the practices as outlined in the (Your league) Coaching guidelines to create a supportive, encouraging, instructional and disciplined environment for all skaters to identify their goals, improve their skating skills and have available all tools necessary to obtain advanced skater status.

H.C. agrees to promote, publicize and strive to increase the visibility of the league through posting and displaying printed (Your League) materials and performingsocial networking management via Facebook,

Twitter, Linked-In, and other online networking and promotional websites.

H.C. agrees to maintain a professional demeanor when acting as a representative of (Your League) and will promote sportsmanlike attitudes and comments towards other leagues and skaters of all affiliations.

H.C. agrees not to utilize shame, humiliation or exercise as punishment for any skater participating in their home league.

H.C. agrees to make deposits to the (Your League) (Your Bank) (or other designated bank) checking account within 3 business days following practice and report all skater attendance, roster and amounts collected within this same time frame.

H.C. will be allowed to choose assistant coaches (1 per team formed) who will be allowed to skate at no charge, and it is the H.C.'s responsibility to see that all assistant coaches follow and agree to the (League Name) policies, procedures, and coaching guidelines.

Signature

Date

Printed Name

Facility Agreement

I understand that (League Name) is a unique (Entity Type) with an emphasis on community. Our mission is to bring Roller Derby to the public as a sport, and work with all participants through communication and the integration of website technology, as well as provide scholarships to skaters for gear, league dues andinsurance.

(League Name) creates value by bringing together community members, leagues, vendors, skating organizations and associations who possess the key ingredients for derby entertainment and exposure to online resources to bring awareness to the public.

Facility Obligations

Engaging in the spirit of community and cooperation in furthering the sport of competitive modern Roller Derby.

I agree to open my facility for the scheduled times for (League Name) practice, and in exchange, I will be given__% of all admission proceeds obtained on behalf of (League Name). I will provide all insurance necessary to operate my facility and will hold harmless (League Name / Facility Name) for any injury or event obtained or incurred while at our facility.

I agree that for any event/bout/game that is scheduled involving my facility, we will incur 1/2 of expenses for marketing and promotion by (League Name) in a mutually agreed upon budget. This budget will be approved and agreed upon 4 weeks prior to the date of the event.

I understand that any and all intellectual property, i.e., marketing materials, curriculum and branding of (League Name), is the property of (League Name),and my involvement is that of a participating facility in the circuit and not one of ownership in any way whatsoever.

(League Name) Obligations

Will provide access to the basic public forum and a private thread for any members/facility.

Will provide all marketing materials, curriculum, accounting, updated weekly roster and skater waivers/paperwork, and coaching staff necessary for the facility to participate in the (League Name).

Provide a link to the facility on our website and will set up a webpage for participating facility upon request.

Will provide a link for t h e facility to sell their merchandise in the League Name shopping cart for an agreed-upon fee to (League Name).

Will schedule events with facility Participation in our scheduled calendar with a mutually agreed upon budget and calendar with all expenses and income to be shared equally. Agreement regarding terms will be signed no later than 30 days prior to scheduled event.

(League Name) will obtain USARS or other insurance with an indemnification rider within 90 days trial period of league startup, as well as additional coverage for any sanctioned event.

Facility membership in the (League Name) may be cancelled or renegotiated witha 30-day notice to (League Name and email)

Facility Member Information

FACILITY NAME:

City of Organization:

Mailing Address:

Phone:

Email Address:

Name of (Contact person and / or League Founder):

Contact Person E-mail:

Phone #: Website URL:

Press Release

The (City) leads the nation by offering Roller Derby as a mainstream sport.

The global Roller Derby explosion has reached Seattle, which now offers the very first recreational City league to form in the Northwest.

(City), (Date);

With Roller Derby growing at a rate of x leagues forming weekly worldwide, (City) is quick to recognize that this is more than just a passing fad. **(League) Roller Derby** is a recreational league now offering classes at the (Location) and even scheduling summer camps for junior skaters. It is also the first (City) area league to open its doors to male skaters of all ages.

Classes are taught through 6-week sessions that are divided into beginning, intermediate and advanced skating levels.

The **_non_**-body contact beginning classes emphasize safety, exercise, basic rules/skating skills and a fun way to socialize.

Intermediate classes graduate to technique work, light hitting drills and endurance, with a focus on positional blocking, scrimmages and team strategies.

Advanced skaters work on hitting drills and scrimmages with positive sportsmanship, teamwork and mentoring as the highest priority. All advanced skaters will have the opportunity to compete on community teams without the standard prerequisite of tryouts and volunteer committee work.

Please view (Website) for more details.

Handout

(YOUR LOGO)

The goal for this six-week session is to prepare you for passing a skills evaluation to be eligible for placement onto a (LEAGUE) team.

All players MUST be wearing full gear at all times while on skates: Mouth guard, helmet, elbow pads, wrist pads, and knee pads. Outdoor wheels are for outdoor skating only. Please make sure you have indoor wheels prior to attending practices.

Skills Before Drills!

(LEAGUE) practices are for teaching/improving skill, agility and endurance levels. Skaters wishing to be on (LEAGUE) teams may attend advanced practices with the coach's assessment and intermediate skills. Advanced practices will progress to positional blocking and full hitting groups & scrimmages.

Skills required for advanced practices will be taught and include:

- Skating posture / Skater Stance
- Stride
- stops
- Crossovers
- Turns
- Speed and endurance
- Falls
- Balance and agility, weaving/proper weight transfer

All skaters are asked to use the (LEAGUE) Forum. Here is how:

- Our website: (WEBSITE)
- Our Forum: From the above website, click the "forum" tab. You will need to login to join. Choose "dues trade" if you are registered through (NAME) College or the City of (NAME).
- Registration at the (LEAGUE) website will not

automatically register you for the forum.

- Please review us at (WEBSITE) and plug-in "Roller Derby" as your search. Please sign up and leave a review!
- A team is only as good as its weakest skater.
- Advanced skaters are expected to mentor/acknowledge weaker skaters.
- Weaker skaters are expected to ask for help and understand that advanced skaters work hard to get skills…do not resent them.
- (Your League) skaters are team players.

Emergency Contact Form

PLEASE FILL OUT THIS FORM, PLACE IT IN A QUART-SIZED ZIP LOCK BAG, AND LEAVE IT IN YOUR GEAR BAG AT ALL TIMES.

FULL (LEGAL) NAME:

SKATER NAME-*OPTIONAL*:

EMERGENCY CONTACT #1 NAME AND PHONE NUMBER

EMERGENCY CONTACT #2 NAME AND PHONE NUMBER

EMERGENCY CONTACT #3 NAME AND PHONE NUMBER

TODAY'S DATE

PLEASE LIST ANY AND ALL MEDICAL CONDITIONS THAT YOU HAVE THAT YOU ARE AWARE OF:

PLEASE LIST ALL MEDICATIONS AND SUPPLEMENTS THAT YOU USE:

YOUR DOB

INSURANCE CARRIER / NUMBER / GROUP NUMBER:

Sponsorship Welcome Letter

Welcome to (LEAGUE)

On behalf of our skaters, referees, Non-Skating Officials and Volunteers, thank you! We are deeply grateful for your interest and support in our league and the (LEAGUE)community.

(LEAGUE) is on a mission — that is to contribute to personal health and wellness for all participants by creating a safe environment to learn, increase self-confidence, realize potential, make social connections and experience overall growth through the sport of Roller Derby with an emphasis on sportsmanship, positive attitudes and athleticism.

Thanks to your generosity, we are able to continue to grow, excel and reach our goals not only for our league, but our skaters and derby family. Without our sponsors this feat would be a difficult one.

Our commitment to you is to bring your company exposure and business, from both our fan base and our derby community over the next year.

We look forward to working with you during this time and seeing you at our games and events.

Again, we cannot thank you enough, and as we say here at (LEAGUE) — Derby Love! If you have questions or comments for (LEAGUE), please feel free to contact us at anytime.

Contact Information

Sponsorship @ (LEAGUE EMAIL)ADDRESS

CITY (WEBSITES)

Sponsor a Skater Contest

Everyone is encouraged to participate – This includes skaters on teams not yeton teams, refs and NSO!

We have made it easy for any business, small or large, who wants to sponsor a skater!

Here are the "sponsor a skater" packages:

- $25 Your logo and link on your favorite skaters' page
- $50 Your logo, link and (Your League) shirt
- $75 Your logo, link, (Your League) Shirt and game ticket
- $100 Your logo, link, (Your League) shirt and 2 game tickets
- $150 Your logo, link, (Your League) shirt, 2 game tickets and recognition at a game/ event

Here is how this will work –

Any skater that brings in a sponsor between $25 - $150

will receive that sponsor's logo/link on their Skater/Bio page and the possibility of wearing that sponsor's logo on your shirts, jerseys, etc.

There will be two prizes awarded –

- Person with the most logos/sponsors brought in by "sponsor a skater."
- Person with the most money brought in by "sponsor a skater."

You will be provided with all the materials needed to participate, answer potential sponsor questions, sign agreements, etc. And, of course, the sponsorship committee is here to help you along the way.

Rules

Contest will run between (DATE) *to* (DATE). Any sponsors collected or signed before or after these dates will not apply to your total count.

All signed sponsor agreements and payment must be turned into to the sponsorship committee no later than (DATE) 11:59 pm.

Sponsors must be an active business that wishes to advertise their products on your skater page/Bio page.

In some cases, you may be asked to wear your sponsors logos on your team/game shirts.

Prizes

Prizes are to be determined and announced based on the number of sponsors brought in. The more we bring in, the bigger the prizes will be!

Sponsorship Levels

Cosmos $2000 Cash Sponsorship	<ul><li>Featured on the (LEAGUE) home & sponsor page with logo & link</li><li>Full page in programs for every game & event of the season</li><li>Company Logo on all posters, flyers, etc.</li><li>8 VIP season tickets (transferable)</li><li>Banners at each game & event (provided by sponsor)</li><li>Company table at each game/event (to be staffed by your company)</li><li>$150 (LEAGUE) Merchandise</li><li>Recognition & announcements throughout each game & event</li></ul>

Starting and Coaching a Roller Derby League

Universe $1000 Cash Sponsorship	• Featured on the (LEAGUE) home & sponsor page with logo & link • 1/2 page in programs for every game & event of the season • Company Logo on all posters, flyers, etc. • 6 VIP season tickets (transferable) • Banners at each game & event (provided by sponsor) • Company table at each game/event (to be staffed by your company) • $100 (LEAGUE) Merchandise • Recognition & announcements throughout each game & event
Global $500 Cash Sponsorship	• Featured on (Your League) sponsors page with logo & link • 1/4 page in programs for every game & event of the season • Company Logo on all posters, flyers, etc. • 4 VIP season tickets (transferable) • Banners at each game & event (provided by sponsor) • $75 (Your League) Merchandise

	• Recognition & announcements start, halftime & end of games
Continent $250 Cash Sponsorship	• Listing on the (LEAGUE) sponsors page with logo & link • 1/8 page in programs for every game & event of the season • Company Logo on all posters, flyers, etc. • 2 VIP season tickets (transferable) • Two (LEAGUE) T-Shirts • Recognition & announcements start & end of games
Sponsor a Skater $25 and Up** Cash Sponsorship	• $25 Your logo and link on your favorite skater's page • $50 Your logo, link and (LEAGUE)shirt • $75 Your logo, link, (LEAGUE) Shirt and game ticket • $100 Your logo, link, (LEAGUE) shirt and 2 game tickets, skater wears your logo • $150 Your logo, link, (LEAGUE) shirt, 2 game tickets, skater wears your • logo and recognition at game/event

General Sponsor a Skater Info

WHY SPONSOR A (LEAGUE) SKATER?

(LEAGUE NAME)

Contact us at Sponsorship@email.com. Learn more about us at www.website.com. Skater/Ref/NSO Name.

Our goal is to teach the necessary skills to anyone who wishes to learn the sport of Roller Derby. We'd like all members of the community to have another venue for exercise, increased self-esteem, social outlets and increased fitness levels. Our leagues are open to women, men, coed and junior skaters of every skill level and our beginning practices aren't full contact; instead, the focus is on core strength, agility and skill building. Once skaters achieve appropriate skill levels, they are allowed to attend our advanced practices and then find the opportunity to skate on a team at public events.

We don't believe that Roller Derby should be limited to women or flat track only. Our affiliate associations are (Association) for banked track and (Association) for flat track. Your contribution will help revolutionize this fast growing sport to mainstream.

The growth of (LEAGUE) will allow us to earmark a percentage of profits to contribute to Head High as well as other community cause's such as childhood obesity and domestic violence awareness. We will continually expand our online networking resources, league growth and make a difference in the sport of Roller Derby.

We have made it easy and inexpensive for you to get your name out there with your favorite skater, which will not only support (LEAGUE) but help generate business for you.

Below, you will find an outline of the different levels we have available for the "Sponsor a Skater" program.

Sponsor a Skater

$25 and Up**

Cash Sponsorship

$25 Your logo and link on your favorite skaters page

$50 Your logo, link and (LEAGUE) shirt

$75 Your logo, link, (LEAGUE) Shirt and gameticket

$100 Your logo, link, (LEAGUE) shirt and 2game tickets, skater wears your logo

$150 Your logo, link, (LEAGUE) shirt, 2 gametickets, skater wears

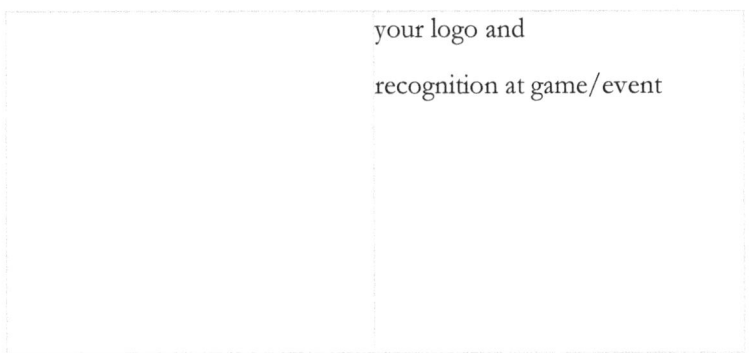

your logo and

recognition at game/event

Contact us at Sponsorship@email.com Learn more about us at www.website.com. Skater/Ref/NSO Name.

(LEAGUE) offers other sponsorship opportunities in addition to the "Sponsor a Skater", which allows advertisement at different levels on our website, programs, fliers, posters, etc.

Please ask your favorite skater for more information, or contact us at Sponsorship@email.com.

Proposals and Marketing

In a perfect world, we would all have a grant writer at our disposal.

Program partners are out there, but I couldn't find one, so I'm including a sample of a successful proposal that I wrote for the City of Seattle Parks Department. This proposal also worked to begin teaching derby classes at North SeattleCollege as well as the City of Bellevue (with revisions, of course).

To get started on your proposal, first do some planning and gather yourinformation. Think about things like:

- What you are looking for? Is it funding, or are you looking for a facility to skate in?
- What kind of support you need?
- Your timeframe: How fast do you want something to happen? Do you want this next month or next year?

- Who might be a good fit in your community as a possible funder?

- Clarify your mission and how you will benefit the community and sponsor.

- How much and what you need?

Start by stating the problem that needs to be addressed in the current situation. Tailor it to your audience and make sure you have supporting evidence to backup your claims. Describe your project in detail; Be Specific! Can you measure your results? (see the survey at the beginning of the book.) Consider taking a survey of your skaters' attitudes about exercise and/ or self- esteem and see if they will agree to answer itquarterly. You can PROVE that this sport will make people's lives better. Are your goals achievable and realistic?

My Junior skating program (before I became too busy with the adult league and handed it over to someone else) was going to launch an off-skates program that could benefit many people. *Included in the curriculum in the worksheets for that and would love to see it put to use for kids anywhere. Use my work and statistics! Create something where there isn't anything. Overall, you need:

- A title page
- An Executive summary
- A Narrative: Keep it clear and simple, avoid acronyms or jargon. Begin with an outline that names your project. Use action words,
- What you need
- A Description of your project
- Information about your organization
- A Conclusion
- Your Budget
- Supporting Materials

Sample Proposal

Table of Contents
1 Current Situation..
2,3,4,5
2
Solution..
6
2.1 Objectives..6
2.2 Approach..6
2.3 Benefits 6
3   Implementation
Plan 6
3.1 Methodology..6
3.2 Administrative..7
3.3 The Program 7
3.4 Qualifications..7
4
Conclusion ....
7
5
Conclusion ....
8
Appendix A: Examples of Appendices..
7,8

Roller Derby is quickly growing in popularity, with over _____ leagues forming weekly across the globe.

Current Situation

The city of_____ does not have any Roller Derby leagues or Roller Derby venues for community members. Roller Derby Leagues in neighboring cities such as _____, _____, and _____ have thriving Roller Derby communities with sold-out venues or standing room only as commonplace occurrences. The sport of modern competitive Roller Derby is experiencing an unparalleled phenomenon with explosive growth throughout the world, and community leagues are extremely limited in their scheduling options. Roller Sports programs, in general, are crowded and popular in today's economy.

Our leagues are currently offering classes through the _____ Parks andRecreation Department as well as _____ College.

Our off-shoot _____ Junior Roller Derby is blossoming with theBoys and Girls Club as a program partner to _____. On October 3rd, 20xx, our fall quarter class at _____ college enrolled 27 skaters. Thefollowing day at _____ Community Center, 25 more skatersattended, bringing the total of new skaters to _____, which was over 50 in twodays.

Our April quarter brought 20 new skaters to our league. Essentially, this was accomplished with the college mailer and our league website/Facebook advertising, with no other means of getting the word out, so it is assumed that thenumbers could increase greatly with a proper marketing strategy. Our East Roller Derby League, on average, brings in 10 new skaters monthly.

There are over x Roller Derby leagues forming weekly across the globe, yet the opportunity to learn the sport in the City of _____ and surrounding areas is, again, quite limited. Roller Derby, as a sport in general, has not been an option for the residents of this city. The average community member wishing to skate or experience team sports such as Roller Derby, roller hockey or speed skating has had difficulty in finding options. Roller Derby alone couldattract many members as currently, it is difficult for the average person if they are unable to make tryouts or have the required commitment or skill level to participate in a competitive league. Roller Derby has an Olympic Committee and is now beta testing those rules, and (Our League) skaters are active participantsin this testing.

It is proposed that a skating program be developed and managed by our league through the _____ Parks Department to pioneer the mainstreaming of this newest Olympic Sport as well as offer an outlet for community members to have yet another exercise and fitness option with the added bonus of being a unique and "alternative" sport. The proposed program will be implemented at the South _____ community center. Roller Derby and other skating programs through our partnership could be offered to the community in a smooth and easily implemented transition.

There are three Roller Derby leagues in (City Name) at this time: X, Girls FlatTrack Roller Derby for women only, Y (Banked Track Roller Derby for women only) and Z Roller Derby, which is our league for women, men, co-ed and Juniors). X and Y have privately rented warehouse space in _____ for practice. Our _____ Roller Derby holds classes at the (Our Town) Community Center and rents the banked track from the Y League. We are currently working to partner with the City of (Our Town) to utilize and/or manage a facility that will be open to the public for roller skating and other roller sports in addition to hosting our Roller Derby practices. W Roller Derby and K Roller Derby (both our leagues) are now forming for public competition in the early 20__. (City name) has a league called _____ Roller Girls, which is a parent group

Starting and Coaching a Roller Derby League

for_____ roller girls for girls ages 8-17. (City name) also has a junior derby group named _____ who practice at the _____ and _____. Both junior leagues are members of the JRDA, which is a fast-growing nationwide association for Junior Derby.

(League X) originally practiced at the roller rink in _____, whichclosed in 20__. Following the closure of the _____ Roller rink, League Xcreated a following by holding events at the _____ facility while practicing at roller skating rinks in _____ and _____.

In the span of six years, League X has grown to have a following that led to thesale of thousands of tickets to their championship event at _____ in 20__.

League Y has completed building their banked track but was previously practicing on a flat track by renting the roller rink at the _____. They were also traveling out of state to practice on a banked track.

Currently, there is a group called Group ZZZ who skate together (mostly) in preparation for trying out for one of the two competitive leagues that are currently available; this group, with approximately 60 members, rents space from as well as from the roller rink in _____.

There are currently over _____ Roller Derby leagues worldwide, and over _____ of them are members of WFTDA, the Women's Flat Track Derby Association, _____ are WFTDA Apprentice Leagues, _____ OSDA; Old School Derby Association, MADE; Modern Athletic Derby Endeavor, _____ CWRDA; Canadian Women's Roller Derby Association, _____ UKRDA; United Kingdom Roller DerbyAssociation, _____ MRDA; Men's Roller Derby Association and_____ JRDA; Junior Roller Derby Association. (add any others that currently exist)

The tidal wave of popularity in Roller Derby is phenomenal and has grown faster than any other grassroots sport to date. The _____ leagues hold dual membership with OSDA for banked track and MADE for flat track competition.

The rate at which leagues are forming is estimated at x% annually, according tostats unofficially maintained at derbyroster.com. In 20__, there were

Starting and Coaching a Roller Derby League

approximately _____ Roller Derby leagues, by 20__, the number climbed to xx, 20__ there were _____ listed on the roster, and to date_____, though allleagues have not been reported. Although the current number of participating athletes in the sport is very small (estimated at under 100,000 participants) incomparison to other more established segments of the team sports industry, the numbers are staggering. No other sport in the world is experiencing this level ofgrowth as they have reached their mature stages of market saturation and fanbase growth.

Based on demographic research conducted by the Women's Flat Track Derby Association, the demographics of Roller Derby skaters within this member organization are as follows: (update these numbers)

98% are female

63% between the ages of 25 and 34.

Average skater age is 31

28% are older than 35

76% consider themselves straight

24% consider themselves gay, lesbian, or other

31% have children under the age of 18 in their

household

25% have some college education

25% have a bachelor's degree

10% have some graduate school education

20% have a graduate degree

60% of skaters spend over $500 annually on Roller Derby-related purchases. The average amount spent by skaters on Roller Derby in 2009 was $966

Additional demographic data provided by the WFTDA study summarizes the profile of Roller Derby fans as follows:

Overall, 59% of derby fans are female versus 41% male

10% of fans are 24 years of age or younger

Fans that are 24 years of age or younger were 83% female to 17% male

41% of the total fans are between 25 and 34

40% of the total fans are between 35 and 55

7% of fans are over 55

The average age of Roller Derby fans is 36

80% fans identify themselves as straight

20% identify themselves as gay, lesbian or other

Starting and Coaching a Roller Derby League

37% are single, 37% are married, and 16% live with a partner

24% have children under 18 in their household

61% have some college education

34% of fans that attended college earned a bachelors degree

30% of fans that attended college went on to graduate school

21% of fans that attended college received a graduate degree

31% of fans have household incomes exceeding $75,000 annually

Avid fans (attending 3 or more bouts per year) have average household in- comes exceeding $65,000 annually and spent $323 on Roller Derby related purchases in 20___.

90% of fans hold a favorable view of local business sponsors

80% of avid derby fans go out of their way to patronize local business sponsors

60% of fans are also fans of traditional major team sports such as baseball, football or basketball

The current stereotypical image of a "hard-partying" roller girl is not the imagethat more athletic participants necessarily wish to have, nor is it the standard the Junior Derby Skaters should hold as an image to strive for and emulate, but until the sport is accepted as mainstream, this stereotype will be hard to break. The current leagues in our area, as well as many across the world, are working hard to change the public perception of the sport being a "spectacle" rather than a sport.

While on a quest to locate a facility to hold our league practices as we built membership, we came to realize that we couldn't find a facility within the city limits of either _____ or _____, other than a short time frame of one two-hour weekly practice at _____. There was not a single school, community center, hall or building available for us to rent until _____ gave us the go-ahead to rent their gymnasium. When posing his dilemma to other leagues nationwide in an online forum, the general response was to "just find any gym or community center which all cities have". Apparently, and _____ are both unique in this lack of available space.

The current private leagues in our area build their entities through volunteer committees that are comprised of skaters. In order to continue membership, skaters must volunteer a minimum number of hours as well as pay monthly dues to participate in their leagues.

Solution

The solution is to offer more classes for recreational Roller Derby leagues and general fitness skating programs that focus on safety, fun and all-inclusiveness. Other future potential recreational skating programs that could benefit or be held by our instructors would be speed skating, skating lessons or open public skating. As Roller Derby gains in popularity and becomes more of an accepted mainstream sport, _____ and _____ are both now on target to be a pioneer in bringing this sport into the mainstream. Our Roller Derby league has been teaching classes through the Parks and Recreation Department since March 2011 at the _____ in addition to having access to the private rental of the facility. During the Summer of 20 __, _____ College also started offering classes at the _____ location.

Program Partner

By working together with us to offer a facility through

the City of _____, we will be able to share a program that will bring fitness opportunities to the community as well as be an overall benefit to the city.

Another bonus would be the visibility and favorable response by the public for being on the cutting edge of mainstreaming the sport of Roller Derby and addressing the needs of community members to access other fitness venues.

An outline of drills and coaching is provided for our coaches with emphasis on agility, strength and repetition of basic skills.

Objectives

Create a venue for Roller Derby classes, public skating, and core strength fitness classes while working towards a future skating facility offering continuous, measurable growth and membership participation.

Our league has also established a 501(c)(3) entity with the State of _____ called the _____ Junior Roller Derby, whose mission is to provide Junior Roller Derby as well as other exercise programs for children, including specialized groups for obese or non-athletic children, and classes open to all children; roller sports and off skates as well.

Approach

We will offer several classes for all Community members at a facility to bedetermined for flat-track Roller Derby skating and/or banked-track skating. Marketing materials will be provided by Our league and The City of _____. We will additionally promote the classes through our website and other social networking resources. The curriculum is provided by Our League.

Benefits

There will be immediate benefits for the community members and the City of _____ with little preparation other than standard inclusion in our combined marketing materials. Other benefits include: bringing an innovative, cutting-edge sport and fitness outlet to the communitywith a tremendous potential for growth and expansion due to the popularity of roller sports.

Marketing

A membership and sponsorship drive, when appropriate to the scheduling of classes, will include the following:

Poster Distribution

Incentive Memberships

Grassroots Social Networking and blogging

Print Advertising

Press Releases

Media Coverage

Administrative

Our League can provide forms, waivers, registration and *USARS insurance information for all registrants and/or work with the City of _____ as an instructor.

The Program

A dynamic coaching style will be introduced, and all coaches will be required to follow our league philosophy of positive communication, encouraging peer-to-peer mentoring and goal setting for personal member achievement. Skills before drills are the credo for our leagues, with an emphasis on sportsmanship and athleticism. Mentorship alliances are also strongly encouraged.

A curriculum with an outline of drills and coaching is provided to our coaches withemphasis on agility, strength, endurance and self-confidence through repetition of basic skills. Attached is a sample of our coaching manual.

Qualifications

(Me) CEO and founder of (Your League) is a veteran of the sport of modern competitive Roller Derby (her avocation) and is striving to make a difference for people and the sport of Roller Derby overall by implementing leagues in (My state) and beyond that are accessible to any individual wishing to experience the many benefits that participation brings.

As the founder and designated broker of one of the more successful real estate sales / residential property management companies in (My State), (Mycompany) (me again) skated in her spare time while also raising her special needs son, now 13 years old (Obviously your own blurb).

(Me) is now the founder and Designated Broker of (My company) in (My town) (My website) and owns and manages a Real Estate brokerage with a property management portfolio. In 20 (Me) founded three fast-growing (League Name) leagues: (League 1) for flat and banked track, (League 2) Roller Derby and (League 3) Roller Derby / (Name) as a sister league.

(Name) currently coaches (My city) Roller Derby League Classes at (My city) Parks Department, (My league) advanced practices, (My town) Community College Roller Derby classes and Junior Derby classes through the (My city) Parks Department. (Name) as also serves as the president of the Old School Derby Association housed in Philadelphia. OSDA has been primarily an East Coast Organization with goals for growth to the West Coast, a goal that they believe (Name) will facilitate.

Prior to skating Roller Derby, (Name) spent most of her life playing softball in competitive leagues and, in the past, served as a volunteer coach for R.U.G Little League, (neighborhood) Community Center girls softball league and (neighborhood) Little League.

Conclusion

(City) is in need of an innovative new alternative to current athletic programs and should consider jumping onto the tidal wave of growth of Roller Derby to accommodate a very fast-growing population of derby enthusiasts.

Bringing more roller sports programs to the community could not only be a popular decision for the City of (name) and members of the community, it would be a cutting-edge statement by recognizing Roller Derby as a mainstream activity while offering other more mainstream activities at the same time.

Having a positive, healthy, fitness-oriented approach to exercise, roller sports and Roller Derby can help change the stereotypical image that has been associated with Roller Derby thus far and can help open doors to unleash the potential of becoming a city-wide activity with participating teams from every community.

Appendix A: Examples of Other Derby Leagues

(Derby as emerging sport)

(Name)

Website: (Website)

Company Overview:

(Mission of league)

(Name)

Website: (Website)

Company Overview:

(Mission of league)

Flat Track Roller Derby is quickly gaining popularity and recognition nationwide. There are over (x) adult women's leagues in the United States and as many as (x and still growing) Junior Roller Derby Leagues are cropping up around the country. Roller Derby is here to stay!

Add testimonials and other information.

Statement of Qualifications

(Attach when proposing a class to your parks department)

Your Name / Your League

1. General Information

(NAME) is an x-year veteran of the sport of modern competitive Roller Derby, previously skating with (LEAGUE) and (LEAGUE). In 20xx (NAME) founded (LEAGUE) with leagues in (CITY) and (CITY). Currently, the (CITY) Roller Derby League skates for two hours each Tuesday night at (location) and is unable to secure additional practice time due to scheduling. Last month, our (CITY) membership grew by ten new skaters, bringing the total to an overall xx skaters.

Our 1st and 2nd ticketed events beginning in January of 20xx sold approximately 300 tickets both times, and our 3rd game is scheduled for April 29th 20xx, at (Location) at 6:30 pm.

Your League

Your address and Info

Company Website:

(Your website) andCommunity Forum:

Telephone:

Toll Free:

Toll Free Fax:

2. Course Information

(CITY) Roller Derby: Skating Classes for all skill levels, designed to teach beginners how to skaters, and overall focus on agility, fitness, confidence and endurance as skills increase. Reasonable course fees are $60-$80 for a 6-8week program or drop-in fees of $10 per session.

3. Qualifications

(NAME); CEO and founder of (LEAGUE) is an xx year veteran of the sport of modern competitive Roller Derby (her avocation) and is striving to make a difference for people and the sport of Roller Derby overall by implementing leagues in (Your area) and beyond that are accessible to any individual wishingto experience the many benefits that participation brings.

In 20xx (NAME) founded three fast-growing (Circuit) leagues: X Roller Derby for flat and banked track, Y Roller Derby and Z Roller Derby / xyxy as a sister league.

(NAME) currently coaches (NAME)Roller Derby League Classes at (CITY) Parks Department, (LEAGUE) advanced practices, (LOCATION) College Roller Derby classes and Junior Derby classes through the (CITY Parks Department. (CITY) Junior Roller Derby is a separate 501C3 founded by (Name) and is based on the model of athleticism and coaching as outlined by (Name) Leagues. (Name) also serves as the president of the (Association) housed in (CITY). (Association)) has been primarily an East Coast Organization with goals for growth to the West coast, a goal that they believe (Name) will facilitate.

Prior to skating Roller Derby, (Name) spent most of her life playing softball on competitive leagues and in the past served as a volunteer coach for (NAME) little league, (NAME) Community Center girls softball league and (NAME) Little League.

4. References

(Name)

(Name)

(Name)

Memorandum of Agreement

between

(CITY) Parks and Recreation

Adult Sports & (CITY) Roller Derby

This Memorandum of Understanding (referred to herein as "MOU") is entered in this _____ day of _____, 20XX by and between (CITY) Roller Derby, a non-profit organization (referred herein as "XXX"), and the (CITY) Department of Parks and Recreation (referred herein as "YYY"), a department that is a part of and an affiliate of the municipal government formally known as The City of (CITY) (the "City").

Recitals.

WHEREAS, there is no ongoing opportunity to play or learn Roller Derby offeredby YYY, and

WHEREAS, XXX is an independent, volunteer-run, 501(c)3 non-profit, recreational Roller Derby league dedicated to athleticism and Roller Derby education and has been training skaters to play and officiate Roller Derby since 2010, and

WHEREAS, YYY serves thousands of people living within the Greater (CITY) Area and connects them to recreational and sport activities throughout the City of (CITY), and

WHEREAS, YYY is dedicated to achieving racial and social equity, including expansion of recreational programs and opportunities for women and LGBTQ adults, and reducing financial barriers to participation in recreation, and

WHEREAS, XXX serves the athletic needs of adult women and LGBTQ individuals, and offers the least expensive opportunity to learn and play Roller Derby in the Greater (CITY) Area, and

WHEREAS, XXX has adequate physical space that can be made appropriate for playing Roller Derby, therefore

NOW, by the mutual covenants and conditions of this MOU, both parties hereby agree to the following:

1. Purpose.

The purpose of this MOU is to formalize terms to

provide training, instruction, and recreation in Roller Derby through SPR programming and facilities and led by XXX managers and instructors. (CITY) Parks and Recreation: (NAME)Community Center (YYY) and (CITY_ Roller Derby (XXX) are entering into this memorandum of agreement to provide training in CO-ED Roller Derby to the residents of Greater (CITY) Area, with the long term goal of lowering the barrier of entry to Roller Derby. Neither agency has the capacity to implement this program independently. YYY has facilities but no programming or expertise in Roller Derby. XXX has expertise and programming but no facilities of its own and does not have the financial capacity to serve low-income skaters without this agreement.

2. Definitions.

A. (ASSOCIATION):

B. New Skater: from XXX, a skater who has not passed minimum skillsqualifications.

C. Team skater: skaters who have passed the (ASSOCIATION) minimum skills qualifications, and who commit to long-time participation with XXX; no minimum attendance is required. Team skaters have access to all practices and scrimmages.

D. Practice: dedicated time to learn and exercise skills and drills from managers and instructors.

E. Scrimmage: dedicated time to practice the rules and game of Roller Derbyin an informal setting.

3. Roles and Responsibilities.

A. XXX shall:

i. Organize a training program for new skaters to improve their skills and knowledge, with the goal of meeting (ASSOCIATION) minimum skills and the skill-set to join a Roller Derby league, if they choose.

ii. Invite coaches from the various leagues to be guest lecturers for skaters. All volunteer lecturers will sign-in on YYY Volunteer Log Sheet, to be provided by YYY staff at each practice.

iii. Maintain (ASSOCIATION) safety standards in regards to "base practices", "games" and "scrimmages";

iv. Insure the practices and naming the City as co-insured, and provide insured personnel responsible for managing all practices.

v. Provide opportunities to practice playing Roller

Derby for newer skaters, skaters in the skill-building part of their career, and skaters who want to skate recreationally.

vi. Train new Roller Derby officials, including referees and non-skating officials (NSOs), to (ASSOCIATION) Rules and Regulations and (ASSOCIATION) Officiating Code of Conduct.

vii. Allow XXXs core skaters to continue to participate to any and all practices by paying monthly membership fee.

viii. Be open to the public to provide a thorough training program. This training program will be in accordance with (ASSOCIATION) safety standards and XXX gender and age policies.

ix. Improve access to low to no-cost Roller Derby training to those who qualify, including expanding the gear loaning program to lower initial financial costs to enter a Roller Derby.

B. SPR shall:

i. Provide exclusive access to the (NAME) Community Center gym that arescheduled in conjunction with other YYY programs and rentals.

ii. Promote the practices and scrimmages to YYY customers. This includes, but is not limited to: quarterly brochures, YYY social media, and on-site flyers and handouts.

iii. Assist XXX staff to complete required Washington State background checks.

iv. Provide appropriate storage space for Roller Derby equipment.

v. YYY is responsible for safety and maintenance of the building.

vi. Provide, collect, and retain concussion and medical waivers of all skaters. This includes YYY sports participation waivers as well as copies of XXX participation and liability forms.

vii. Register skaters into the YYY registration system and collect fees at the time of registration. With the intent to maintain a familiar structure as when XXX operated solely:

a. Core skaters will register on a monthly basis, in alignment with XXX's previous dues schedule.

b. New skaters and public drop-in participants

may pay a single-practice fee without registration.

viii. Provide YYY managers and staff with updated registration sheets.

ix. Assist participants with the Parks scholarship application in order to provide low- to no-cost access to YYY programs, including XXX Roller Derby.

4. Benefits of the MOU.

A. SPR will be able to offer a unique recreational sport through a high-qualityservice provider, SRD, not previously offered in this capacity.

B. Financial access to Roller Derby sports is improved, as SPR has the financialcapacity to support low-income skaters.

C. Addition of a sport to YYY that is pro-LGBTQ and Co-ed-focused,achieving goals of the Race and Social Justice Initiative.

5. Similar Activities.

This MOA in no way restricts YYY or XXX from participating in similar activities with other public or private agencies, organizations, and individuals.

6. Amendments.

This MOU may be modified or amended by written agreement among the two parties of this MOU.

7. Termination and Cancellation.

YYY or XXX may terminate this Agreement for convenience by thirty (30) days written notice to the other party. YYY may terminate this MOA if XXX is in material breach of any terms of this Agreement, and such breach has not been corrected to YYY's reasonable satisfaction in a timely manner. This MOU will expire one year from the date of execution unless renewed by mutual agreement of both parties. If either party exercises its right not to renew the MOU upon expiration, three month's notice is required.

This partnership agreement will be effective upon both parties signing the MOU, and will be null and void on: December 31, 20___.

8. Nondiscrimination and Equality of Treatment.

A. XXX will comply with all applicable equal employment opportunity and nondiscrimination laws of the United States, the State of (STATE), and the City of (CITY), including but not limited to Chapters (#), and 2(#) of the (CITY)Municipal Code (YMC), as they may be amended; and rules, regulations, orders, anddirectives of the associated administrative agencies and their officers.

B. XXX shall conduct its business in a manner that assures fair, equal, and nondiscriminatory treatment at all times, in all respects, to all persons in accordance with all applicable laws, ordinances, resolutions, rules, and regulations.

C. YYY acknowledges XXX's gender policy and that there is full access to all practices, to be scheduled by XXX and advertised by SPR.

Failure to comply with any of the terms of these provisions shall be a material breach of this MOU.

9. Damage or Destruction

10. Indemnification

Both Parties agree to defend, indemnify, and hold each other harmless from any and all claims, suits, actions, costs and damages of any nature whatsoeverarising from either party's actions and performance of this MOU, including third-party claims that may arise and levied against either party. Such indemnification shall survive the term of this MOU.

XXX agrees to hold YYY harmless from any claims that may arise as a result of the implementation of this agreement unless such claims have been determined tobe the sole negligence or wrongful conduct of YYY. The indemnification proclamation and agreement in this provision shall be effective through the termof this MOU and any further extension thereof. SRD will have its own liability insurance and volunteers shall sign SPR volunteer sign-in sheets.

11. Contacts

The principal contacts for this agreement are:

(NAME), Director, Recreation Division, (CITY) Parks and Recreation

(NAME) Manager, Special Units

(NUMBER) NAME@CITY.gov

(NAME), Recreation Program Coordinator, Adult Sports

Name:

Skater Application & Waiver

Date of birth: email: Phone:

Current address:

City: State: ZIP Code:

EMERGENCY CONTACT

Name

Address: Phone:

City: State: ZIP Code:

Relationship:

Medical: It is the responsibility of the undersigned to ensure that the above-named person is medically fit to participate in strenuous on-rink or off-rinkactivities. As stated below, participation in Roller Derby activities presents an inherent risk of injury to a person or property. The undersigned certifies that the above-named participant has no known conditions that prohibit or limit participation in any derby/skating activities held by or in association with our member leagues (including its facilities, officers, agents, investors and advisors). Additionally, the undersigned must have medical insurance in place for the participant to cover any expenses related to any potential injury that may arise from their participation in the leagues.

Equipment and Skates: Participants must wear the following mandatory safety equipment during all skating activities: Knee, Elbow and Wrist Pads and a Helmet and mouth guard. Eyeglasses must have plastic shatterproof lenses. The undersigned must take full responsibility that the above named participant (including self) is wearing the aforementioned safety equipment at all times and that it is properly worn. Only Quad roller skates are permitted. All skates must be track-safe, meaning that their use must not gash, indent or blemish the skating surface or any other surface and that the skates will not cause injury to propertyor person(s). All liabilities thereof are undertaken by the undersigned.

Conduct: Spectators (patrons on the premises as a result of your involvement in skating practice, public appearances, fundraising activities or any other sanctioned league events, as well as participants, must behave in a respectful manner to both person and property. Behavior that could potentially lead to intentional or unintentional bodily injury or injury to property willnot be tolerated.

Indemnification and Risk Acknowledgment: In consideration of being allowed to participate in any way in league sports programs, related events and activities, including, but not limited to: training sessions, team meetings, public appearances, fundraising activities or travel to and from any league related events, the undersigned acknowledges, appreciates and agrees that:

The risk of injuries from the activities involved in this program is significant,including the potential for permanent paralysis and death, and while particular rules, equipment and personal discipline may reduce this risk, the risk of serious injury remains.

I KNOWINGLY AND FREELY ASSUME ALL SUCH RISKS, both known and unknown, EVEN IF ARISING FROM THE NEGLIGENCE OF THE RELEASEES or others, and I assume full responsibility for my participation;

and,

I willingly agree to comply with the stated and customary terms and conditions for participation. If, however, I observe any unusual significant hazard during my presence or participation, I will remove myself from participation and bring suchto the attention of the nearest official immediately;

and,

I, for myself and on behalf of my heirs, assigns, personal representatives and next of kin, HEREBY RELEASE AND HOLD HARMLESS any league member league, the hosting facility, the rinks, coaches, their officers, officials, agents, and/or employees, other participants, sponsoring agencies, sponsors and advertisers ("RELEASEES") WITH RESPECT TO ANY AND ALL INJURY, DISABILITY, DEATH, or loss, or damage to person or property, WHETHER ARISING FROM THE NEGLIGENCE OF THE RELEASEES OR OTHER-WISE.

I acknowledge that I have received a copy of the league member Policies, and I do commit to read and follow these policies. I am aware that if, at any time, I have questions regarding league policies I should direct them to my head coach or the Administrative offices.

I grant all leagues and affiliate partners the right to use my photograph, likeness, video or voice recording with or without my name for broadcast or publication in any and all media. I hereby release any claims of copyright, slander, violation of privacy or similar rights that I may have. There is not an expiration date on this release. I will not seek compensation for usage.

I know that league policies and other related documents do not form a contract of any kind and are not a guarantee by this league of the conditions and benefitsthat are described within them. Nevertheless, the provisions of such leaguepolicies are incorporated into the acknowledgment, and I agree that I shall abide by its provisions. I also am aware that this league, at any time, mayon reasonable notice, change, add to, or delete from the provisions of the company policies.

I HAVE READ THIS ASSUMPTION OF RISK AGREEMENT, ACKNOWLEDGMENT, AND I ACCEPT RESPONSIBILITY; I FULLY UNDERSTAND ITS TERMS, AND I UNDERSTAND THAT I HAVE GIVEN UP SUBSTANTIAL RIGHTS BY SIGNING IT, AND I SIGN IT FREELY AND VOLUNTARILY WITHOUT ANY INDUCEMENT.

SIGNATURES

Name of applicant:

Date:

Signature of PARENT OR GUARDIAN (IF UNDER 18):

Date:

Applicant Signature (if over 18)

Date:

Starting and Coaching a Roller Derby League

| TEAM PLACEMENT EVALUATION | PAGE 1 |

PLEASE PUT SKATER NAME ON EVERY PAGE AT TIME OF EVALUATION

| NAME: | DATE INITIATED:
 DATE APPROVED: | LOCATION: |

I - POSTURE

A. SKATERS STANDS WITH KNEES FLEXED, FEET SHOULDER WIDTH APART
Head and Chest up

| NEEDS WORK ○ | ALMOST THERE ○ | SKILL ACHIEVED ○ |

B. CAN ROTATE HEAD AND SHOULDERS 360 DEGREES WHILE IN STANCE
Adjusting quickly to cues

| NEEDS WORK ○ | ALMOST THERE ○ | SKILL ACHIEVED ○ |

C). PERFORMING THE ABOVE WHILE ROLLING
Consider previous experience and correct posture as needed, allow skaters to find balance on each foot - forward and both feet -backward

| NEEDS WORK ○ | ALMOST THERE ○ | SKILL ACHIEVED ○ |

II - FALLS AND SLIDES

A. SINGLE KNEE SLIDES BOTH LEFT AND RIGHT
1). Sliding to a stop with upper body in control without hands touching floor at any time

| NEEDS WORK ○ | ALMOST THERE ○ | SKILL ACHIEVED ○ |

SINGLE KNEE SLIDES BOTH LEFT AND RIGHT
2). Knee Touches (touch and go) with quick recovery

| NEEDS WORK ○ | ALMOST THERE ○ | SKILL ACHIEVED ○ |

B. DOUBLE KNEE SLIDE TO A STOP
Keeping upper body in control without sitting back onto skates

C. FIGURE 4 FALL / SOFTBALL SLIDE
1). Skater remains in control as legs form the shape of a number 4, lowering the body onto the floor, rolling onto ones side with legs and arms "tucked in" to "fall small"
2). Can recover in 3 seconds from tucked position

| NEEDS WORK ○ | ALMOST THERE ○ | SKILL ACHIEVED ○ |

revised December 2011

| TEAM PLACEMENT EVALUATION | | PAGE 2 |

PLEASE PUT SKATER NAME ON EVERY PAGE AT TIME OF EVALUATION

SKATER NAME:		LOCATION:

II FALLS AND SLIDES – Continued

D. 180 DEGREE KNEE SLIDE, BOTH LEFT AND RIGHT
1). Skater performs knee slide, then accomplishes a turn of 180 degrees before the slide comes to an end.
2). Upper body stays in control, the foot of the knee sliding leg is moved forcefully across the back of the body to create momentum to create the turn

NEEDS WORK ⃝	ALMOST THERE ⃝	SKILL ACHIEVED ⃝

III -STOPS

A. BASIC T STOP
Slip or drag of a foot to bring one to a stop

NEEDS WORK ⃝	ALMOST THERE ⃝	SKILL ACHIEVED ⃝

B. PLOW STOP
Begin using 1 foot to slide at 45 degree angle to the skating foot, then adding 2nd foot to the slide to a complete stop

NEEDS WORK ⃝	ALMOST THERE ⃝	SKILL ACHIEVED ⃝

C. HOCKEY STOP
Sliding sideways on skates, both directions

NEEDS WORK ⃝	ALMOST THERE ⃝	SKILL ACHIEVED ⃝

IV -STEPPING

WITHOUT ROLLING THE WHEELS OF THE SKATES, THE SKATER WILL BE ABLE TO DEMONSTRATE THEIR COMFORT WITH THE BODY'S BALANCE POINT BY STEPPING SIDEWAYS, BOTH DIRECTIONS, FORWARD, AND BACK-

NEEDS WORK ⃝	ALMOST THERE ⃝	SKILL ACHIEVED ⃝

V –SKATING

A. CORRECT POSTURE IS KEY
B. BODY IS LEANING LEFT, INTO THE CIRCLE, TILTING SHOULDERS, BUT NOT TWISTING THE BODY

NEEDS WORK ⃝	ALMOST THERE ⃝	SKILL ACHIEVED ⃝

revised December 2011

Starting and Coaching a Roller Derby League

TEAM PLACEMENT EVALUATION

PAGE 3

PLEASE PUT SKATER NAME ON EVERY PAGE AT TIME OF EVAULATION

SKATER NAME:	LOCATION:

VI – CROSSOVERS

A. CROSSOVERS
Skater performs smooth crossovers skating at a brisk pace, into, around and out of corners

NEEDS WORK ◯	ALMOST THERE ◯	SKILL ACHIEVED ◯

B. CROSSOVERS
Body is leaning left, into the circle, tilting shoulders but not twisting the body

NEEDS WORK ◯	ALMOST THERE ◯	SKILL ACHIEVED ◯

C. CROSSOVERS
Skater uses both feet to push for power during crossovers

VII SPEED AND ENDURANCE

SKATER CAN COMPLETE 5 LAPS IN ONE MINUTE
On Usars Regulation Track

NEEDS WORK ◯	ALMOST THERE ◯	SKILL ACHIEVED ◯

SKATER COMPLETES 25 LAPS IN 5 MINUTES
USARS REGULATION TRACK

NEEDS WORK ◯	ALMOST THERE ◯	SKILL ACHIEVED ◯

VIII HOPPING AND JUMPING

JUMPING WHILE ROLLING FORWARD
Landing on both feet simultaneously, should be able to clear 3" obstacle

NEEDS WORK ◯	ALMOST THERE ◯	SKILL ACHIEVED ◯

HOPPING FROM ONE FOOT TO THE OTHER
And back again several times while rolling

NEEDS WORK ◯	ALMOST THERE ◯	SKILL ACHIEVED ◯

revised December 2011

Donna Kay

TEAM PLACEMENT EVALUATION

PLEASE PUT SKATER NAME ON EVERY PAGE AT TIME OF EVALUATION

SKATER NAME:		LOCATION:

IX SQUATS WHILE ROLLING

A. Skaters should be able to complete a complete squat, with buttocks lowered all the way to the heels

NEEDS WORK ○	ALMOST THERE ○	SKILL ACHIEVED ○

B. THE SKATER MUST BE ABLE TO GAIN SPEED (Using scissor / all 8 wheels) on ground No hands on the floor, and control direction of travel through the use of shoulder leans

NEEDS WORK ○	ALMOST THERE ○	SKILL ACHIEVED ○

X MANEUVERABILITY AND AGILITY

A. MANEUVER THROUGH CONES, PLACED 4-5 FEET APART AROUND THE TRACK AT A BRISK SPEED

NEEDS WORK ○	ALMOST THERE ○	SKILL ACHIEVED ○

B. SKATER MUST BE ABLE TO MOVE QUICKLY FROM THE INSIDE CIRCUMFERENCE OF THE TRACK, TO THE OUTSIDE BORDER OF THE TRACK, AND BACK AGAIN, USING A COMBINATION OF SLIDES, STRIDES AND CROSSOVERS

NEEDS WORK	ALMOST THERE ○	SKILL ACHIEVED ○

C. SKATER CAN TRANSITION FROM FORWARD TO REVERSE SKATING WHILE AT A BRISK PACE *OWRD– NOT USARS REQUIREMENT*

NEEDS WORK	ALMOST THERE ○	SKILL ACHIEVED ○

C. SKATER CAN MONKEY ROLL (from a brisk pace fall small to both knees, elbows and wrist on the ground and roll WITH the momentum returning quickly to "start" position *OWRD– NOT USARS REQUIREMENT*

NEEDS WORK	ALMOST THERE ○	SKILL ACHIEVED ○

revised December 2011

Starting and Coaching a Roller Derby League

TEAM PLACEMENT EVALUATION

PAGE 5

PLEASE PUT SKATER NAME ON EVERY PAGE AT TIME OF EVALUATION

SKATER NAME:	LOCATION:

IX ASSISTS

A. Skaters should be able to offer an assist (whip) to another skater by extending right arm towards outside line, utilizing upper body momentum (shifting weight) and shoulders to propel teammate forward while remaining in a sturdy skater stance

NEEDS WORK ◯	ALMOST THERE ◯	SKILL ACHIEVED ◯

B. Skaters should be able to receive the above to gain forward speed and momentum while remaining in control of stride and stance.

NEEDS WORK ◯	ALMOST THERE ◯	SKILL ACHIEVED ◯

B. SKATERS CAN GIVE AND RECEIVE HIP WHIPS

NEEDS WORK ◯	ALMOST THERE ◯	SKILL ACHIEVED ◯

B. Skaters should be able to offer an assist while skating in reverse direction by pulling arms in towards waist, to either side. *^OWRD AllStar Requirement*

X PUSHES AND HITS

A. SKATER CAN PUSH ANOTHER SKATER OUT OF BOUNDS (BOTH TO INSIDE AND OUTSIDE LINES) WITHOUT GOING OUT OF BOUNDS

NEEDS WORK	ALMOST THERE ◯	SKILL ACHIEVED ◯

B. SKATER CAN GIVE HIP CHECKS AND SHOULDER CHECKS ON BOTH SIDES WITHOUT LOSING BALANCE OR CONTROL

NEEDS WORK ◯	ALMOST THERE ◯	SKILL ACHIEVED ◯

C. SKATER CAN RECEIVE HIP CHECKS AND SHOULDER CHECKS WITHOUT LOSING BALANCE OR CONTROL

NEEDS WORK ◯	ALMOST THERE ◯	SKILL ACHIEVED ◯

TRAINER NAME:_____

TRAINER SIGNATURE_____ revised December 2011

DATE:_____

About the Author

Donna 'the hot flash' Kay is a veteran of the modern competitive Roller Derby; she originally skated with Rat City Roller Girls and Tilted Thunder Rail Birds in Seattle, starting at the age of 48 as a beginner. After around four years, the skills "started clicking," and she became excited to share what she had learned and went on to found Seattle Roller Derby, Bellevue Roller Derby, and OneWorld Roller Derby.

She worked to implement the first Roller Derby program in the city of Seattle as a city-run league. As chair and member of the USA Roller Sports national Roller Derby committee in Lincoln, NE, Donna began her quest to mainstream the sport of Roller Derby. In addition to coaching her own teams and leagues, her experience includes conducting skill-based workshops for six years' at Rollercon, an annual international Roller Derby convention that hosts thousands of national and international Roller Derby athletes.

Donna started the Facebook group 'Derby Over 40' (now known as Roller Derby Over 40) and an inspirational website showcasing skaters over the age of 40. Follow the links to learn more about the sport:
https://thehotflashseattle.wordpress.com
https://www.skaterollerderby.com/

www.ingramcontent.com/pod-product-compliance
Lightning Source LLC
Chambersburg PA
CBHW070350120526
44590CB00014B/1084